THRIVING THROUGH ADOLESCENCE : A CONCISE HEALTH GUIDE

DR. AALIYA TABASUM
DR. BABAR ZARGAR

Contents

Preface

This book provides an in-depth exploration of adolescent health, covering physical, mental, emotional, and social aspects in a structured manner. Backed by extensive research, it references both Indian and international studies, journals, and expert opinions. It takes a holistic approach to well-being by addressing nutrition, physical fitness, sleep hygiene, mental health, self-esteem, and stress management. Practical strategies and real-life applications are included to help adolescents implement self-help techniques in their daily lives. Additionally, the book tackles modern-day challenges such as digital well-being, cyber safety, social media influence, peer pressure, and career readiness. Written in an engaging and accessible style, it is suitable for adolescents, parents, educators, and healthcare professionals. Each chapter includes key takeaways that summarize essential concepts for quick reference. The book also offers step-by-step guidance on goal setting, time management, and decision-making to empower adolescents in shaping their future. Emphasizing mindfulness and emotional resilience, it promotes mental well-being through mindfulness techniques, meditation, and stress management practices. Designed for academic and practical use, it is an ideal resource for schools, counselling sessions, parenting guides, and adolescent education programs, making it a must-read for anyone looking to navigate the challenges of growing up successfully.

Acknowledgements

The journey of creating *Thriving Through Adolescence: A Concise Health Guide* has been both enlightening and fulfilling. This work would not have been possible without the support, insights, and dedication of many individuals to whom I am deeply grateful.

First and foremost, I extend my heartfelt appreciation to my family for their unwavering encouragement, patience, and understanding throughout this endeavour. Their support has been the foundation of my academic and professional pursuits.

A special mention goes to my son, Abdullah whose keen interest, insightful discussions, and continuous motivation have played a significant role in shaping this book. As he himself transitions into adolescence, his perspectives have provided a deeper understanding of the challenges faced by young individuals today, enriching the content of this guide in a meaningful way.

A profound note of appreciation is extended to my esteemed co-author, Dr. **Babar**, whose expertise, dedication, and collaborative spirit have been invaluable in bringing this book to fruition. His contributions, drawn from his vast knowledge and clinical experience, have enriched the depth and breadth of this guide, ensuring its comprehensive and practical approach to adolescent health.

I am immensely grateful to my esteemed colleagues, mentors, and students at **Government Medical College, Doda**, for their valuable insights, professional guidance, and constructive discussions, which have greatly enhanced the quality and relevance of this book. Their contributions have been instrumental in ensuring that this guide serves as a reliable resource for adolescents, parents, and educators alike.

I also extend my sincere gratitude to the **Federation of Obstetric and Gynecological Societies of India (FOGSI)** for its relentless commitment to advancing adolescent health and medical education. Their ongoing efforts in this field continue to inspire and guide our work.

Furthermore, I acknowledge the contributions of researchers, scholars, and healthcare professionals whose work has provided the scientific foundation for this book. Their dedication to adolescent health has been instrumental in shaping the perspectives presented here.

Lastly, my deepest appreciation goes to the readers—students, educators, healthcare professionals, and young minds—who inspire the creation of meaningful literature. It is my sincere hope that this book serves as a valuable resource in navigating adolescence with confidence, awareness, and well-being.

With deepest gratitude,
Dr. Aaliya Tabasum

CHAPTER I

UNDERSTANDING ADOLESCENCE

Adolescence is a time of transition—one of the most intricate and changing periods in human growth. Lasting from approximately ages 10 through 19, adolescence is a time when the body, mind, and social world are dramatically changing. It can feel like an overwhelming process, but it also sets the stage for the rest of your life. In order to really succeed during adolescence, it's critical to know what's occurring at a biological, emotional, and psychological level.

The Stage of Development of Adolescence

Adolescence is different from childhood and adulthood. It is characterized by a mixture of physical development, emotional growth, and cognitive changes. This stage is a transition between the carefree period of childhood and the responsibility and independence of adulthood. Even though this stage in life is usually known to occur between the ages of 10 and 19, the adolescence experience may be quite different among individuals.

Physically, adolescence is defined by puberty, a series of biological changes that initiate growth spurts, sexual development, and brain structure changes. These are difficult to handle and can result in a range of emotional reactions, including more mood swings, greater sensitivity and self-consciousness.

Physical Changes and Puberty

Puberty is the biological development that signals the onset of adolescence. It is fuelled by hormonal fluctuations that impact the body and brain. In girls, puberty usually starts between 8 and 13 years of age, and in boys, between 9 and 14 years of age. The body experiences a series of physical changes during this period, including growth spurts, the emergence of secondary sexual features (e.g., breasts in females and facial hair in males), and shifts in body composition.

These bodily changes while a natural process of maturation, tend to be awkward or confusing. The increase in growth and weight, for instance, can make one feel disproportionate, and hormonal changes can influence skin, mood, and energy level. Allowing adolescents to know that the changes are temporary and are part of normal development can make them feel more confident at this stage.

The brain itself also changes in profound ways in adolescence. The prefrontal cortex, which is the region of the brain involved in decision-making, control of impulses and reasoning matures more slowly than other regions of the brain, including the limbic system, which handles emotion and reward. This unequal development can help to account for why teenagers may have strong emotions or have trouble making thoughtful choices. But this is a stage of brain development, and eventually, the prefrontal cortex matures so that better self-regulation and decision-making abilities can occur.

Emotional and Psychological Development

The emotional changes that are witnessed in adolescence can be as strong as the physical transformations. This is also a time of seeking identity, independence and self-exploration. Teenagers start to shift away from their parents as significant influences and move towards accepting their peers. This desire for peer acceptance can at times result in high-risk behaviour or poor choices, as teenagers tend to value belonging more than other considerations.

In addition, emotional susceptibility is heightened in adolescence. The brain's increased sensitivity to rewards and social stimuli makes teens more prone to experiencing strong feelings of happiness, sorrow, or rejection. Mood swings, unstable self-esteem, and heightened sensitivity to criticism are all common in teens. These ups and downs of emotions can be overwhelming, but they are all part of the natural process of building emotional intelligence and resilience.

Adolescence is also a period of identity and value exploration. During adolescence, individuals are likely to wonder who they are, where they fit in, and what they desire from life. This is essential in establishing a solid sense of self that will inform decision-making and relationships long into adulthood. Although this time of self-discovery can be confusing, it is to be expected as a part of development. The confusion that so often comes with adolescence sets the stage for a clearer sense of identity in later years.

The Role of Social and Peer Relationships

Social relationships become more significant to an individual's sense of self-worth and happiness during adolescence. Friendships also become more complicated, and peer influence becomes a dominant force for shaping attitudes and behaviours. At this time, most teenagers start to feel the pressure of conforming, whether it involves what they look like, what they wear, or how they behave. Peer pressure is a strong force, sometimes having people do things that they otherwise might not consider.

But adolescence is also a time to establish significant, meaningful relationships with others. Friendships at this stage of life tend to be centred around common interests, respect for each other, and emotional support. These friendships are potential sources of strength and positive reinforcement as the adolescent copes with the experiences of growing up. It's important to be able to spot healthy friendships, establish boundaries, and learn how to say no when peer pressure results in unfavourable consequences.

The Significance of Family Support

Even as peer relationships gain centre stage, family remains important in the life of an adolescent. Teenagers might crave greater autonomy from their parents, but they continue to require their support, advice and care. An appreciation for the tension between independence and family ties is the secret to a successful adolescence.

Throughout this chapter, the one thing that needs to be understood is that parents and teenagers will inevitably develop a different relationship. The quest for independence might bring about disagreement or miscommunication, but respectful communication and good communication are key to sustaining a solid family unit. Parents and caregivers can also play a big role in assisting teenagers through the difficulties of maturing.

Preparing for the Transition to Adulthood

Adolescence is ultimately about preparation for adulthood. The experiences, choices, and lessons learned during this time can shape who you become as an adult. The skills developed—such as emotional regulation, decision-making, problem-solving, and self-reflection—will serve you well as you enter adulthood. While adolescence can sometimes feel uncertain or difficult, it is also a time of great potential. With the right support and self-awareness, this can be a period of immense personal growth.

Recognizing the biological, emotional, and social shifts of adolescence is the key to surviving this stage. In the subsequent chapters, we will explore the particular areas of adolescence—mental health, relationships, school struggles and so on—giving you the information and strategies to succeed during this formative period.

CHAPTER II

THE ADOLESCENT BRAIN

Adolescence is a period of rapid brain growth, and understanding these changes can help in overcoming the challenges of growing up. During this phase, the brain undergoes significant transformations that influence decision-making, emotions, and social interactions. This chapter explores these changes and their effects on behaviour, thinking, and life experiences.

Contrary to popular belief, brain development does not stop at puberty. In fact, adolescence is a crucial time of rapid neural growth. The brain continues to develop into early adulthood, with the most significant changes occurring in two key regions: the **prefrontal cortex** and the **limbic system**.

The Prefrontal Cortex: *The Centre of Reasoning and Decision-Making*

The prefrontal cortex is responsible for higher-order thinking, such as planning, reasoning, and decision-making. It also plays a key role in impulse control and behavioural regulation. However, during adolescence, this region is still developing and has not yet reached full maturity. This is why teenagers may sometimes act impulsively or make decisions that seem irrational. It's not that they are incapable of making sound choices, but rather that their brain is still building the capacity to fully assess long-term consequences and make well-thought-out decisions.

The Limbic System: *The Emotional Centre*

The limbic system is responsible for emotions, motivation, and reward processing. It develops faster than the prefrontal cortex during adolescence, leading to heightened emotional responses. This imbalance between emotional and rational processing often results in intense feelings, mood swings, and risk-taking behaviour.

Why Teens Take Risks

One of the most fascinating aspects of the adolescent brain is its heightened sensitivity to rewards. The limbic system is more active in teenagers, particularly when seeking new, exciting, or stimulating experiences. This increased sensitivity explains why adolescents are more likely to engage in risk-taking behaviours—whether it's trying something new, seeking approval from peers, or testing boundaries.

Since the prefrontal cortex is still developing, teenagers tend to prioritize short-term pleasures over long-term outcomes. Being aware of this can help in understanding impulsive actions and decision-making patterns.

Emotions and the Teenage Brain

Adolescence is often an emotionally intense period. Changes in the limbic system make it easier to experience extreme highs and lows. One moment, you may feel immense happiness, and the next, frustration or sadness. These emotional fluctuations are completely normal and are a natural part of brain development.

Teenagers also tend to be highly sensitive to social experiences, such as peer pressure, romantic relationships, and rejection. While this heightened sensitivity allows for greater social awareness, it can also lead to feelings of being misunderstood or overwhelmed.

The Impact of Sleep on Brain Development

Sleep plays a crucial role in brain development during adolescence. Changes in the body's internal clock (circadian rhythm) naturally make teenagers want to stay up later and wake up later. However, school schedules and societal demands often disrupt this pattern, leading to sleep deprivation.

Lack of sleep affects brain function, impacting memory, decision-making, and emotional regulation. Studies show that inadequate sleep can disrupt emotional processing and cognitive performance. Prioritizing sufficient rest is essential for managing stress, staying focused, and maintaining emotional stability.

The Role of Experience in Brain Development

The adolescent brain is highly adaptable and shaped by experiences. What you do, think, and feel directly influences brain growth. Positive experiences—such as mindfulness, healthy social relationships, and learning new skills—enhance brain development. On the other hand, negative influences like chronic stress, trauma, or poor sleep habits can make it harder to regulate emotions and make sound decisions.

This is why adolescence is a critical time for developing good habits. The choices made during these years help strengthen neural connections, leading to a more resilient and well-functioning brain in adulthood.

Tips for Supporting Brain Development

- **Prioritize Sleep**: Aim for 8–10 hours of sleep each night to allow your brain to rest and recover.
- **Challenge Your Brain**: Engage in activities like reading, puzzles, or learning new skills to stimulate brain growth.
- **Manage Stress**: Practice relaxation techniques, such as meditation and deep breathing, to reduce stress and improve emotional health.
- **Make Thoughtful Decisions**: Recognize that your brain is still developing—it's okay to make mistakes, but learn from them.

Conclusion

The adolescent brain undergoes significant changes that shape thoughts, emotions, and behaviours. Understanding these changes can foster greater self-awareness and emotional intelligence. While some aspects of teenage behaviour may seem challenging, they are all a natural part of brain development. Embrace this phase, knowing that as your brain matures, you will gain greater control over your choices, emotions, and actions.

HORMONAL AND PHYSICAL CHANGES

Introduction

Adolescence is a transformative period marked by significant hormonal and physical changes. These changes are primarily driven by the endocrine system, which regulates growth, development, and reproductive functions. The onset of puberty initiates a cascade of hormonal shifts that lead to the development of secondary sexual characteristics, alterations in body composition, and emotional fluctuations. Understanding these changes is essential for navigating adolescence with awareness and confidence.

The Role of Hormones in Adolescence

Hormones are chemical messengers produced by endocrine glands that influence various physiological and behavioural processes. During adolescence, several key hormones drive puberty and physical maturation.

1. Gonadotropin-Releasing Hormone (GnRH)

The hypothalamus releases gonadotropin-releasing hormone (GnRH), which signals the pituitary gland to secrete luteinizing hormone (LH) and follicle-stimulating hormone (FSH). These hormones regulate the function of the gonads (testes in males and ovaries in females), leading to increased production of sex hormones.

2. Testosterone and Estrogen

Testosterone and estrogen are the primary sex hormones responsible for the development of secondary sexual characteristics. While both males and females produce these hormones, testosterone levels are significantly higher in males, while estrogen levels are predominant in females.

- **Testosterone** promotes muscle growth, deepens the voice, stimulates facial and body hair growth, and plays a role in sperm production.
- **Estrogen** stimulates breast development, regulates menstrual cycles, influences fat distribution, and contributes to bone health.

3. Growth Hormone (GH)

The pituitary gland secretes growth hormone (GH), which is crucial for increasing height and muscle mass during adolescence. GH stimulates bone elongation and contributes to overall physical development.

4. Adrenal Hormones

The adrenal glands produce androgens, which contribute to the development of pubic and underarm hair in both sexes. They also influence skin changes, such as increased oil production leading to acne.

5. Thyroid Hormones

Thyroid hormones regulate metabolism, energy levels, and overall growth. Imbalances in thyroid hormone levels can affect weight, mood, and cognitive function during adolescence.

Physical Changes During Puberty

The hormonal surge during adolescence leads to significant physical transformations. These changes occur at different rates and times for individuals but generally follow a predictable pattern.

Growth Spurt

One of the most noticeable changes during puberty is the rapid increase in height and weight. This growth spurt occurs earlier in females, typically between ages 10 and 14, while in males, it usually happens between ages 12 and 16. Growth plates in long bones elongate due to increased GH production, contributing to height gain.

Development of Secondary Sexual Characteristics

Secondary sexual characteristics are physical traits that distinguish males from females but are not directly involved in reproduction.

- **In Males:**

  - Enlargement of the testes and penis
  - Deepening of the voice due to vocal cord thickening
  - Growth of facial, chest, and body hair
  - Increased muscle mass and broader shoulders

- **In Females:**

  - Breast development
  - Widening of hips for potential childbearing
  - Growth of pubic and underarm hair
  - Onset of menstruation (menarche)

Changes in Body Composition

Hormonal fluctuations lead to shifts in body composition. Males tend to develop more lean muscle mass and reduced body fat due to the effects of testosterone. In contrast, females experience an increase in body fat, particularly in the hips, thighs, and breasts, as estrogen prepares the body for reproductive functions.

Skin and Hair Changes

Sebaceous (oil) glands become more active due to androgen stimulation, leading to increased oil production and a higher likelihood of acne. Hair growth patterns also change, with pubic, underarm, and facial hair appearing in males and pubic and underarm hair developing in females.

Voice Changes

In males, the larynx (voice box) enlarges, causing the voice to deepen. This process is often accompanied by voice cracks as the vocal cords adjust to their new structure. In females, vocal changes are less pronounced but may involve slight deepening of the voice.

Menstrual Cycle and Reproductive Maturity

For females, the onset of menstruation marks reproductive maturity. The menstrual cycle is regulated by the interplay of estrogen and progesterone, which prepare the uterus for potential pregnancy. Initially, menstrual cycles may be irregular but stabilize over time.

Psychological and Emotional Changes

Hormonal fluctuations also influence emotions and behavior. Adolescents may experience mood swings, heightened sensitivity, and increased emotional intensity due to the interaction between sex hormones and neurotransmitters.

Mood Swings and Emotional Sensitivity

The rise in sex hormones affects brain chemistry, leading to fluctuations in mood. Adolescents may feel euphoric one moment and irritable the next. Understanding these changes can help in managing emotional responses effectively.

Increased Risk-Taking Behaviour

Testosterone and dopamine levels contribute to a heightened desire for new experiences, thrill-seeking, and risk-taking behaviours. While this can foster creativity and independence, it may also lead to impulsive decision-making.

Social Awareness and Peer Influence

Adolescents become more conscious of their social environment, seeking validation from peers. The need for acceptance can influence self-esteem and decision-making, sometimes leading to peer pressure.

Managing the Changes of Adolescence

Understanding and managing these changes can ease the transition into adulthood.

Healthy Lifestyle Habits

- **Nutrition:** A balanced diet rich in protein, healthy fats, vitamins, and minerals supports growth and hormonal balance.
- **Exercise:** Regular physical activity helps regulate mood, maintain a healthy weight, and improve overall well-being.
- **Sleep:** Adolescents require 8–10 hours of sleep per night for proper growth and cognitive function.

Hygiene and Skincare

- **Washing the face daily** can help manage acne by reducing excess oil and bacteria.
- **Using mild skincare products** prevents irritation and supports skin health.
- **Maintaining personal hygiene**, such as regular bathing and using deodorant, helps manage body odor caused by increased sweat production.

Coping with Emotional Changes

- **Mindfulness and relaxation techniques** can help regulate emotions and reduce stress.
- **Open communication** with parents, teachers, or counselors provides support and guidance.
- **Engaging in hobbies and interests** fosters self-expression and emotional well-being.

Conclusion

Hormonal and physical changes during adolescence shape an individual's transition into adulthood. While these transformations can be challenging, they are a natural and essential part of growth. Understanding these changes can empower adolescents to navigate this phase with confidence, embracing their evolving physical and emotional selves. By adopting healthy habits and seeking support when needed, they can foster a positive and balanced development that prepares them for the future.

CHAPTER IV

EMOTIONAL HEALTH

Adolescence is a period of great emotional development and transformation. The emotional hurdles that accompany this stage of life may at times seem overwhelming, but they are absolutely normal. While your body and brain change dramatically, your emotions do too. This chapter will assist you in making sense of the emotional changes you may go through, how to handle them and why it's so vital that you take care of your emotional well-being.

The Rollercoaster of Feelings

If you ever find that your feelings are all over the place, then you know that you are not alone. Being an adolescent is a time of sudden shifts in feelings and sometimes it seems like they're a rollercoaster ride. One day you could be completely on top of the world and the next you may be sad, mad, or frustrated. They are intense and baffling changes, but they are part of the natural progression of your body.

The main cause of these mood swings is the surge in hormones during puberty. Hormones such as estrogen and testosterone have a strong effect on mood, and the area of your brain that manages emotions—the limbic system—is still maturing. This makes it more difficult to control and manage your emotions sometimes. Though these mood highs and lows can be overwhelming, keep in mind that they are a natural process of developing into an adult.

Knowing Mood Swings

Mood swings are normal in teenagers and they occur due to various reasons. As explained above, changes in hormones are one of the key causes of mood swings, but they also relate to other aspects of being a teenager, including:

Stress: School, relationships and other pressures can cause stress, which often triggers emotional reactions.

Social Influence: Your interactions with friends, family and peers can significantly impact your mood. Conflicts, peer pressure, or the desire for acceptance can lead to strong emotional responses.

Identity Formation: Adolescence is a period of discovery and discovering who you are can be thrilling and overwhelming. This process can bring uncertainty and confusion, which can lead to mood swings.

Though mood swings are part of being an adolescent, learning how to cope with them so they don't disrupt your daily life or health is crucial.

Building Emotional Resilience

Emotional resilience is the capacity to deal with stress, disappointments and negative emotions. Acquiring this skill in adolescence is important for your mental and emotional health in the future. Here are a few tips on how to develop emotional resilience:

Self-awareness: Notice how you feel and attempt to see what causes these feelings. Do you feel stressed, anxious, or angry? Knowing what's causing your emotions can help you better control them. For instance, if you realize that you feel frustrated following a difficult day at school, you may be able to determine stress as the underlying cause and do something to deal with it.

Express your emotions: Bottling up your emotions can lead to frustration, anxiety, or even physical tension. It's important to find healthy ways to express what you're feeling. Talk to a trusted friend or family member, write in a journal, or even engage in creative activities like drawing or music to express your emotions.

Practice mindfulness: Mindfulness is the ability to remain in the present moment and aware of what is going on. Practicing mindfulness can calm your mind when you become overwhelmed with emotion. Basic skills such as breathing deeply or meditation with a guide can minimize stress and heighten your emotional perception.

Build problem-solving skills: Becoming able to handle problems in a logical, unemotional manner can make you feel more capable of managing your emotions. Rather than letting problems get the best of you, step back, analyse them and work out practical solutions.

Establish a support network: Having individuals you feel comfortable talking with and relying on is vital for emotional well-being. Whether you have friends, family, or a mentor figure, confiding in them, asking for their advice or a listening ear, can make you feel heard and validated.

Take care of your body: Physical health is closely related to emotional health. Exercise, sleep, and nutrition all affect how you feel emotionally. When your body feels good, your mind is better able to manage the ups and downs of life.

Dealing with Anxiety and Stress

Anxiety and stress are common emotional challenges that many adolescents face. The pressures of school, relationships, family expectations and the social environment can sometimes feel overwhelming. Learning how to manage these emotions is important for maintaining your overall well-being.

Here are some strategies for coping with anxiety and stress:

Take a deep breath: If you feel stressed or anxious, deep breathing has the potential to soothe your nervous system. Practice the "4-7-8 technique": Inhale slowly for 4 seconds through the nose, hold it for 7 seconds and then slowly exhale it for 8 seconds through the mouth. Continue to do it for a couple of cycles so that you reduce your anxiety level.

Stay organized: Keeping track of your responsibilities and tasks can reduce feelings of being overwhelmed. Make to-do lists or use a planner to break down your tasks into manageable steps.

Discuss it: Sometimes talking about what's causing your anxiety can take some of the pressure off. Discuss your concerns with a parent, teacher, or friend. If anxiety or stress are ongoing problems, talk to a mental health professional who can assist you in learning how to cope.

Keep your focus on what you can control: Worrying about the things that are not in your control triggers anxiety. Focus on the current situation and what you can do to mitigate the situation at hand instead of worrying about possible futures.

Coping with Depression

At times, emotions such as sadness can be too much, and you might have symptoms of depression. Depression is not simply being "down" for a couple of days—it's a pervasive sense of sadness or hopelessness that can affect daily functioning.

If you're consistently feeling sad for a long time, you need to talk to someone you feel comfortable with, such as a parent, teacher, or school counsellor. Depression is not a sickness to be ashamed of and there's help out there.

If you find any of these to be true, then get some help:

Being sad or hopeless a lot of the time

Loss of interest in activities that were once pleasurable

Difficulty with sleep (too much or too little)
Having trouble concentrating or making decisions
Worthlessness or guilt
Recurring thoughts about harming oneself or suicide (call for help at once if this is true)

Why Emotional Health Matters

It's equally important to take care of your emotional well-being as your physical well-being. If you know your feelings, know how to deal with them, and are resilient, you'll be more capable of handling the stresses of life in a healthy and positive way. Emotional health has an influence on your relationships, your schoolwork, your body, and overall happiness.

By being self-aware, getting support, and employing coping mechanisms, you can build a solid foundation for emotional health that will serve you well throughout your life.

Adolescence is a period of high emotional development, and it's natural to feel a broad spectrum of emotions. The secret to surviving this stage is knowing your emotions and learning healthy ways to manage them. Keep in mind that you can ask for help when you need it, and you don't have to do this alone. By prioritizing your emotional health, you're creating the strength and resilience necessary to meet life's challenges head-on and become a strong, well-adjusted adult.

CHAPTER V

SOCIAL CONNECTIONS AND RELATIONSHIPS

Adolescence is a critical period for social development, where relationships play a pivotal role in shaping one's sense of identity and emotional well-being. During this phase, young people seek acceptance, belonging, and meaningful connections. Interactions with family, peers, and friends help develop essential life skills such as communication, empathy, and conflict management. However, adolescence also presents challenges such as peer pressure, social comparison, and the growing impact of social media. Navigating healthy relationships during this stage is crucial for long-term emotional and social health.

The social ties formed during adolescence are not only about making friends but also contribute significantly to an individual's self-concept and emotional health. As adolescents explore different social roles, they begin to understand social norms and learn how to regulate emotions within relationships. These relationships offer opportunities to practice empathy, teamwork, and cooperation—skills necessary for personal and professional success in adulthood. Despite this, the period also brings struggles like identity confusion, peer conflicts, and emotional challenges, which can impact an adolescent's social growth if not handled correctly.

Family's Influence on Social Development

Family serves as the foundation for social and emotional growth during adolescence. Teens with strong bonds with their parents or caregivers often experience higher self-esteem, better emotional regulation, and a deeper sense of security. Open communication, mutual respect, and shared experiences help create a supportive environment where adolescents feel safe expressing their feelings. Families play an important role in promoting a positive self-image by offering encouragement, guidance, and emotional support.

However, the adolescent phase can alter family dynamics. As teens seek independence, parents may struggle with balancing autonomy and authority, often leading to misunderstandings, conflicts, and emotional distancing. To navigate this period, it is crucial for parents to engage in open, non-judgmental communication. Shared family activities, such as meals, games, or outings, can help preserve strong family bonds. Studies show that adolescents who feel connected to their families are less likely to engage in risky behaviours and more likely to perform better academically.

Siblings also play an important role in social development. Through interactions, adolescents learn conflict resolution, sharing, and collaboration. Positive sibling relationships provide extra emotional support and companionship, enhancing overall well-being. Even sibling rivalry, if managed well, can help develop important social skills like negotiation and compromise.

Friendships and Peer Influence

Friendships become increasingly important during adolescence, serving as a primary source of emotional support, self-discovery, and social learning. Peers provide companionship, shared experiences, and validation, all contributing to the adolescent's developing sense of self. As teens spend more time with friends than family, peer relationships heavily influence their behaviour and self-concept.

Healthy friendships encourage positive behaviours, including academic focus, extracurricular participation, and empathy development. Teens with strong friendships tend to show better emotional regulation and social skills. On the flip side, negative peer influence can lead to risky behaviours, such as substance use, delinquency, or unsafe online activity. Adolescents under peer pressure may face self-esteem issues or anxiety related to social acceptance.

To help teens navigate peer relationships, parents, educators, and counsellors should teach skills like assertiveness, critical thinking, and boundary setting. Teens must understand that real friendships are based on mutual respect and shared values, not just conformity to peer expectations. Schools can play a significant role in fostering positive peer interactions by organizing support programs, social skills workshops, and peer-driven activities.

The Impact of social media on Relationships.

Social media plays a significant role in adolescent life today. Online platforms provide opportunities for connection, self-expression, and exploration of interests. For many adolescents, social media is a lifeline, especially when face-to-face interactions are limited. It offers a sense of belonging, especially for those feeling isolated in their immediate social circles.

However, social media also introduces challenges. The trend of social comparison, where teens measure themselves against the curated lives of others, can lead to feelings of inadequacy, anxiety, and low self-esteem. Studies show that excessive social media use is linked to higher levels of depression, sleep problems, and body image concerns. The anonymity of online platforms also raises the risk of cyberbullying, which can lead to significant emotional harm.

Parents and educators should work together to educate teens about responsible social media use. Setting time limits, discussing online safety, and encouraging digital detoxes can promote healthier relationships with technology. Teaching teens to critically assess online content and prioritize real-world connections is essential for their overall well-being.

Managing Peer Pressure and Building Healthy Relationships

Peer pressure is a common experience during adolescence, as teens strive to fit in with their peers and gain social approval. While positive peer influence can encourage healthy habits like sports participation and academic engagement, negative peer pressure can lead to risky behaviours such as substance abuse or poor decision-making.

To help teens resist negative peer pressure, it's vital to teach them practical strategies. Encouraging assertive communication, such as confidently saying "no" when necessary, can empower adolescents to uphold their values and make independent choices. Supporting teens in choosing friends who respect their boundaries and share their interests can reduce the likelihood of yielding to harmful peer influence.

Involvement in structured social groups, such as clubs, sports teams, or volunteer organizations, provides positive social environments that promote healthy behaviour. Teens involved in such activities are more likely to engage in constructive pursuits and less likely to be swayed by negative peer groups.

Conflict Resolution and Emotional Intelligence

Conflicts are a natural aspect of any relationship, particularly during adolescence when individuals assert their independence and form their identities. Learning to resolve conflicts in a healthy way is an essential social skill that enhances emotional intelligence and relationship satisfaction. Emotional intelligence, which includes self-awareness, empathy, and emotional regulation, helps teens manage interpersonal challenges more effectively.

Teens with strong emotional intelligence are better equipped to handle disagreements without resorting to aggression or withdrawal. Key conflict-resolution strategies include active listening, calmly expressing emotions, and seeking solutions that benefit all parties. Schools and community programs can promote emotional intelligence by implementing social-emotional learning (SEL) curricula that teach these critical skills.

Conclusion

Relationships play a central role in adolescent development. Strong family connections, supportive friendships, and healthy social media habits contribute to emotional stability and social competence. By understanding relationship dynamics, resisting negative peer pressure, and learning conflict-resolution strategies, adolescents can form meaningful connections that promote their growth and well-being. Through navigating these complexities, they are better prepared to form lasting, positive relationships throughout their lives.

CHAPTER VI

MENTAL HEALTH AND EMOTIONAL WELL-BIENG

Adolescence is a critical period of growth, not only physically but also mentally and emotionally. During this stage, adolescents undergo numerous changes that can significantly affect their mental health and emotional well-being. The pressures of academic success, social expectations, and personal identity development can create both opportunities for growth and challenges that need careful attention. This chapter explores the importance of understanding adolescent mental health, common challenges they face, strategies for emotional regulation, and the role of support systems in ensuring their well-being.

Understanding Adolescent Mental Health

Mental health during adolescence is a vital aspect of overall well-being. Adolescents are transitioning from childhood to adulthood, and their ability to manage emotions, stress, and the complexities of social interactions is being developed. Adolescence is also a time when individuals begin to form their personal identity and navigate their place within society. These tasks can bring about both excitement and anxiety, leading to emotional ups and downs.

During this time, young people may experience a variety of emotions, from intense joy to deep sadness, confusion, and frustration. This is normal, but when these feelings become overwhelming or persist for extended periods, it can signal a mental health challenge. Understanding mental health during this stage is essential, as it allows both adolescents and the adults in their lives to recognize when professional help might be needed.

Common Mental Health Challenges in Adolescence

Adolescents are particularly vulnerable to mental health challenges due to the rapid physical, emotional, and social changes they experience. Among the most common mental health concerns during this period are anxiety, depression, and stress.

1. **Anxiety**: Anxiety is one of the most prevalent mental health challenges among adolescents. It can manifest as excessive worry, nervousness, and fear about events, social situations, or future outcomes. Adolescents may also experience physical symptoms like headaches, difficulty sleeping, or stomach aches. Anxiety often becomes pronounced in situations like exams, social events, or navigating peer relationships, especially in the face of pressure to perform or conform.

2. **Depression**: Adolescents may also face depression, which can present as persistent feelings of sadness, hopelessness, or a lack of interest in activities once enjoyed. Depression can lead to difficulty concentrating, changes in sleep or eating habits, and feelings of worthlessness. Depression can also manifest physically, as a lack of energy or physical discomfort. It is essential to distinguish between occasional sadness and clinical depression, as the latter requires intervention and treatment.

3. **Stress**: The demands of schoolwork, extracurricular activities, peer relationships, and family expectations can all contribute to stress. When stress becomes chronic, it can impact an adolescent's ability to function effectively in daily life. Stress can lead to feelings of being overwhelmed, irritability, difficulty sleeping, and difficulty focusing. Understanding the sources of stress and learning coping mechanisms are crucial for mental health during this time.

Strategies for Emotional Regulation and Resilience

Adolescents often find themselves navigating strong emotions and challenges that can impact their mental health. However, there are effective strategies for emotional regulation and building resilience, which can help young people manage their emotions in a healthy way.

1. **Mindfulness and Relaxation Techniques**: Mindfulness practices, such as deep breathing, meditation, and yoga, can help adolescents regulate their emotions. These techniques promote self-awareness and a calm, cantered state of mind. By focusing on the present moment, adolescents can reduce stress and anxiety and gain a better perspective on their feelings.

2. **Physical Activity**: Regular physical activity plays a vital role in promoting mental health. Exercise releases endorphins, which are chemicals in the brain that help reduce stress and improve mood. Adolescents who engage in physical activities, whether through sports,

dancing, or walking, often experience better emotional regulation and a greater sense of well-being.

3. **Time Management**: Adolescents often feel stressed when faced with multiple responsibilities. Learning time management skills can help them prioritize tasks, reduce procrastination, and feel more in control of their schedules. Setting small, achievable goals and breaking large tasks into manageable steps can help reduce anxiety and prevent burnout.

4. **Building Strong Relationships**: Having supportive relationships with family, friends, or mentors is crucial for emotional well-being. Positive relationships provide adolescents with a safe space to express themselves and feel understood. Communication, trust, and empathy are key components of these relationships, and they can help adolescents cope with difficult emotions or stressful situations.

5. **Developing Positive Self-Talk**: Adolescents often experience negative self-talk that can impact their self-esteem and emotional health. Teaching them how to recognize and challenge negative thoughts and replace them with positive affirmations can improve their emotional regulation. Encouraging a growth mindset, where mistakes are viewed as opportunities for growth rather than failures, is also beneficial.

The Role of Family and School Support Systems
Support systems play an integral role in the mental health and emotional well-being of adolescents. Families and schools are central to providing the guidance, encouragement, and resources needed to help adolescents navigate this challenging period.

1. **Family Support**: Families are often the first line of defence when it comes to supporting adolescent mental health. Open communication, empathy, and understanding create a foundation for emotional well-being. Adolescents should feel comfortable discussing their thoughts, feelings, and struggles with trusted family members without fear of judgment. It is also important for families to recognize the signs of mental health issues, such as changes in behaviour, mood swings, or withdrawal, and seek appropriate help when needed.

2. **School Support**: Schools are another crucial environment for adolescent mental health. Teachers, counsellors, and administrators can help identify mental health challenges early and provide interventions

or referrals to mental health professionals. Schools can also offer programs focused on emotional well-being, mental health awareness, and stress management. Creating a supportive and inclusive school environment can reduce stigma and provide students with the tools to cope with challenges.

3. **Peer Support**: Peer relationships are important for adolescents, and friends can provide valuable emotional support. Encouraging open, honest conversations among peers can help reduce feelings of isolation and anxiety. Peer support groups or mentorship programs can also be effective in creating a sense of community and belonging.

Seeking Help and Reducing Mental Health Stigma

Unfortunately, many adolescents face barriers when it comes to seeking help for mental health concerns. There is often a stigma surrounding mental health that prevents young people from reaching out for support. This stigma can be exacerbated by societal expectations and a lack of understanding about mental health issues.

Educating adolescents, families, and communities about mental health is essential for reducing stigma and promoting mental well-being. Encouraging open discussions about mental health, normalizing the need for support, and offering resources for counselling or therapy can help adolescents feel more comfortable seeking help.

Schools and community organizations can play a key role in reducing stigma by offering mental health education programs and promoting awareness. Mental health professionals, such as counsellors, therapists, or psychologists, can also provide valuable resources and support for adolescents experiencing emotional challenges.

Conclusion

Mental health and emotional well-being are integral aspects of adolescent development. Adolescents face unique challenges that can affect their mental health, but with the right support and strategies, they can learn to manage their emotions and build resilience. Families, schools, and peers play an important role in fostering a supportive environment where adolescents can thrive. By understanding common mental health challenges, learning emotional regulation techniques, and reducing stigma around mental health, we can help adolescents navigate this critical period and set the stage for a healthy, fulfilling future.

CHAPTER VII

DIGITAL HEALTH AND SAFETY

In the digital age, technology has become an integral part of daily life, especially for adolescents. The internet, social media, and mobile applications provide adolescents with vast opportunities for learning, social interaction, and self-expression. However, while the digital world offers significant benefits, it also poses risks to mental, emotional, and physical health. This chapter examines the impact of technology on adolescent health, offers strategies for managing screen time, explores the dynamics of online relationships, and highlights the importance of protecting personal information. By understanding these aspects, adolescents, families and educators can promote safe and responsible digital engagement.

Impact of Technology on Adolescent Health

The rapid advancement of technology has transformed the way adolescents interact with the world around them. Mobile phones, social media platforms and the internet allow for constant connectivity, providing instant access to information, entertainment and communication. For many adolescents, technology plays a central role in their social lives, academic achievements, and personal development.

However, excessive use of digital devices can have negative effects on adolescent health. Studies suggest that prolonged screen time is associated with physical issues like eye strain, poor posture and sleep disturbances. Adolescents who spend a significant amount of time on screens may be at risk for developing sedentary lifestyles, leading to obesity and related health problems. Moreover, technology use can contribute to mental health challenges, including anxiety, depression, and social isolation, particularly when it replaces face-to-face interactions or when adolescents engage in unhealthy online behaviours.

The pressure to maintain a certain online persona, coupled with constant exposure to curated content on social media, can lead to feelings of inadequacy and low self-esteem. Adolescents may compare their lives to the seemingly perfect lives of influencers and peers, resulting in increased stress and body image concerns.

It is essential for parents, caregivers, and educators to help adolescents navigate the digital world in a way that promotes well-being while minimizing the potential harms associated with excessive screen time and online exposure.

Screen Time Management and Digital Well-being

With the increasing amount of time adolescents spend on digital devices, managing screen time has become an important part of promoting their overall well-being. Balancing technology use with offline activities is key to ensuring that adolescents benefit from technology without compromising their physical and mental health.

1. **Setting Boundaries**: One of the first steps in managing screen time is setting clear boundaries around when and how long adolescents can use digital devices. Parents can establish rules for screen time, such as limiting it to a specific number of hours per day or designating certain times, such as during meals or before bed, as screen-free times. This helps ensure that technology does not interfere with important activities like sleep, family time, or physical exercise.

2. **Encouraging Physical Activity**: To combat the sedentary lifestyle associated with prolonged screen time, it is crucial to encourage regular physical activity. Whether through sports, outdoor activities, or simple exercises, physical movement can promote better health and improve mood. Exercise can also help adolescents release built-up tension and reduce stress, which can result from overuse of digital devices.

3. **Promoting Offline Socialization**: While digital devices enable adolescents to connect with others virtually, it is equally important to encourage in-person interactions. Adolescents should be encouraged to spend time with friends and family in real life, whether through outings, social gatherings, or other shared activities. Face-to-face interactions help build communication skills and emotional connections that are vital for healthy social development.

4. **Creating a Healthy Digital Environment**: Encourage adolescents to curate their digital environment in a positive way. This means following accounts and joining groups that inspire creativity, learning, and healthy activities rather than those that promote negative behaviours or unrealistic standards. Parents can guide adolescents in how to use digital platforms in ways that align with their values and contribute to their well-being.

5. **Quality over Quantity**: It is not just the amount of screen time that matters, but also the quality of the time spent. Parents can help their children make thoughtful choices by encouraging them to use technology for educational purposes, creative expression, or connecting with supportive communities. Encouraging balance and mindful use can make technology a tool for personal growth rather than a source of distraction or stress.

Online Relationships and Cyberbullying

As technology has redefined how adolescents communicate, online relationships have become a significant part of their social lives. Adolescents now have the ability to connect with people around the world through social media, gaming platforms, and messaging apps. These relationships can provide a sense of belonging and foster meaningful interactions. However, the digital realm also introduces challenges such as cyberbullying, online harassment, and the potential for risky behaviours.

1. **Cyberbullying**: One of the most concerning issues related to online relationships is cyberbullying. The anonymity provided by the internet can lead to harmful behaviours, where individuals use digital platforms to harass, intimidate, or humiliate others. Cyberbullying can have serious emotional and psychological consequences for adolescents, including depression, anxiety, and even suicidal thoughts.

To combat cyberbullying, it is important to educate adolescents about the risks of online harassment and empower them to act if they experience or witness bullying. Teaching them how to block or report harmful content, encouraging open communication with trusted adults, and reinforcing the importance of kindness and respect online can help prevent cyberbullying.

1. **Online Safety**: Adolescents should be aware of the potential risks of sharing personal information online. When interacting with others on social media or other platforms, they should avoid revealing sensitive details such as their home address, phone number, or passwords. It is also essential to remind adolescents about the importance of protecting their privacy settings and being mindful of who can access their content.

2. **Setting Boundaries in Digital Relationships**: Adolescents need to be taught how to set boundaries in their online relationships, just as they would in their offline relationships. This includes knowing when to disengage from unhealthy or toxic online interactions, recognizing when a relationship is becoming abusive, and understanding the importance of mutual respect.

Protecting Personal Information and Digital Literacy

In the digital age, protecting personal information has become more important than ever. Adolescents often share personal details online, whether in social media posts, online games, or messaging apps, without fully understanding the potential consequences. Educating adolescents about digital privacy and cybersecurity is critical in keeping their personal information safe.

1. **Digital Footprint**: Adolescents should be made aware of their digital footprint—the record of everything they post, share, or interact with online. Anything shared on the internet has the potential to remain accessible long-term, even if deleted. This makes it important for adolescents to think critically before posting or sharing personal information.
2. **Password Management**: Adolescents should be encouraged to create strong, unique passwords for their online accounts and to avoid using the same password across multiple sites. Parents can help them set up password managers to securely store their login information and prevent hacking.
3. **Digital Literacy**: Understanding how the digital world works is an essential skill for adolescents. Digital literacy goes beyond using technology; it involves understanding how information is shared, recognizing misinformation or scams, and identifying the ethical implications of online behaviour. Teaching adolescents to critically evaluate online content and be mindful of what they post, share, and believe is crucial for their safety and well-being.

Positive Use of Technology for Learning and Growth

While there are risks associated with excessive screen time and digital interaction, technology can also be a powerful tool for learning and personal growth. The internet provides an endless array of educational resources, from online courses and tutorials to interactive learning platforms and virtual museums. Adolescents can use technology to explore their interests, enhance their academic knowledge, and develop new skills.

1. **Educational Platforms**: Adolescents can take advantage of online resources that support their academic goals, such as Khan Academy, Coursera, and YouTube tutorials. These platforms offer a wide range of subjects, from science and mathematics to art and literature. Encouraging adolescents to explore subjects outside of their regular curriculum can spark creativity and intellectual curiosity.
2. **Creative Expression**: Digital tools also provide opportunities for creative expression. Adolescents can engage in activities such as photography, video creation, blogging, or coding, all of which can foster their creativity and problem-solving skills. Encouraging adolescents to use technology to create rather than just consume can contribute to a healthy digital experience.
3. **Community Engagement**: Technology enables adolescents to connect with like-minded individuals or groups who share their passions, whether it's through online forums, social media groups, or virtual volunteer opportunities. These digital communities can foster a sense of belonging and provide a platform for positive self-expression.

Conclusion

Technology has transformed the way adolescents live, learn, and interact with the world. While it offers numerous benefits, including access to information, social connections, and creative outlets, it also presents challenges related to physical health, mental well-being, and online safety. By managing screen time, promoting offline activities, and educating adolescents about the risks and rewards of the digital world, we can ensure that technology becomes a positive influence in their lives. Through digital literacy, privacy protection, and healthy online relationships, adolescents can engage with technology in a way that supports their growth and well-being, both online and offline.

CHAPTER VIII

REPRODUCTIVE HEALTH AND PUBERTY EDUCATION

Adolescence is a critical phase of human development, and it marks the transition from childhood to adulthood. This period is characterized by significant physical, emotional, and psychological changes that impact the adolescent's overall growth. Among the most prominent transformations are those related to reproductive health and puberty. These changes are not only biological but also have emotional and social implications for adolescents. Therefore, providing proper education and support during this time is crucial in helping them navigate these challenges and take charge of their health and well-being.

This chapter explores various aspects of reproductive health, including the physical changes during puberty, menstrual health, hygiene management, and the importance of education about reproductive health. It also addresses the myths and misconceptions surrounding puberty and reproductive health, empowering adolescents with accurate knowledge to make informed decisions.

The Importance of Puberty Education

Puberty education plays a vital role in the overall health and development of adolescents. Without proper education, adolescents may feel confused, anxious, or embarrassed about the changes happening in their bodies. Early and accurate reproductive health education helps adolescents to not only understand the physical changes but also manage emotional and social aspects associated with puberty. Such education fosters a sense of confidence and self-acceptance, ensuring that adolescents are well-prepared for the changes that come with puberty.

Puberty education is particularly important because it equips adolescents with the knowledge, they need to make informed decisions about their bodies, health, and well-being. By learning about reproduction, sexual health, and hygiene, adolescents can build healthy habits that will last a lifetime. Moreover, addressing the stigma and shame that sometimes surrounds topics like menstruation and sexual development can create a safe and open environment where adolescents feel comfortable discussing their concerns.

Understanding Puberty and Its Physical Changes

Puberty is marked by rapid physical growth and changes in the body, driven by hormonal shifts. These changes are different for each individual, but the general pattern and timeline remain similar across genders. Puberty typically occurs between the ages of 8 and 14 for girls, and between 9 and 15 for boys. However, the exact age of onset can vary due to factors such as genetics, environmental influences, and nutrition.

For girls, the first sign of puberty is often the development of breast buds, followed by the growth of pubic and underarm hair. These physical changes are accompanied by an increase in body fat, particularly around the hips and thighs, which gives the body a more rounded shape. Around the age of 12 or 13, girls will experience their first menstrual cycle, known as menarche. This marks the beginning of their ability to conceive, although the body is still developing and maturing.

For boys, puberty is marked by the enlargement of the testes and penis, followed by the deepening of the voice. Boys also experience the growth of facial and body hair, increased muscle mass, and broader shoulders. Additionally, there is an increase in the production of sperm, which allows boys to father children. The development of sexual characteristics in boys and girls occurs due to changes in the levels of sex hormones—estrogen in girls and testosterone in boys.

During puberty, adolescents experience growth spurts, during which they may rapidly gain height and weight. These changes can sometimes be disorienting as the body adjusts to new proportions. Additionally, the skin undergoes changes, with many adolescents developing acne due to increased oil production. This is a common and temporary condition that typically resolves after puberty.

Although the physical changes of puberty are often discussed in terms of sexual maturity, they are also an essential part of overall growth. Puberty is not just about reproductive capacity; it is a critical period in which adolescents develop the physical and emotional strength to thrive as adults.

Emotional and Psychological Changes During Puberty

In addition to physical changes, puberty also brings emotional and psychological changes. These can be just as intense and challenging as the physical transformations. Adolescents often experience mood swings, which are partly due to hormonal fluctuations, but they are also influenced by the social pressures and emotional challenges that come with adolescence.

The desire for independence and autonomy grows stronger during puberty. Adolescents may begin to question authority figures, assert their opinions, and challenge family rules. This is part of their development of a personal identity and a sense of self. At the same time, they may also feel uncertain about their place in the world and experience feelings of loneliness, self-doubt, and confusion.

The growing awareness of sexual attraction also plays a significant role in adolescent development. As adolescents become more aware of their sexuality, they may experience sexual desires, fantasies, and curiosity. This can lead to confusion, especially if they do not have the proper guidance and support. It is essential to address these feelings and provide accurate, age-appropriate education about sexuality, relationships, and consent.

Adolescents are also navigating a complex social world during puberty. Peer relationships become more important than ever, and social acceptance can play a significant role in self-esteem. Adolescents may feel pressure to conform to peer expectations, whether related to appearance, behaviour, or sexual activity. This is a time when peer influence, both positive and negative, can significantly impact the choices that adolescents make.

Menstrual Health and Hygiene Management
Menstruation is one of the most significant milestones in a girl's life, marking the start of her reproductive potential. However, it is also a time when many girls face confusion, embarrassment, and challenges related to menstrual health. Menstrual health education is essential for helping girls understand what to expect, how to manage their periods, and how to maintain hygiene during menstruation.

Menstrual cycles typically occur every 28 days, though cycles can range from 21 to 35 days. A normal menstrual period lasts between 3 and 7 days, during which the body sheds the lining of the uterus. It is important for girls to know that menstrual cycles may be irregular in the first few years after menarche and that this is completely normal. As their bodies continue to develop, cycles generally become more regular.

Education about menstrual hygiene is also critical. Using sanitary products like pads, tampons, or menstrual cups correctly ensures that girls maintain proper hygiene and comfort during their periods. It is essential to emphasize the importance of changing sanitary products regularly to prevent infections and maintain overall reproductive health. Girls should also be educated about the importance of washing hands before and after changing menstrual products to reduce the risk of infections.

Girls should be taught to track their menstrual cycles, as this can help them identify any irregularities that may require medical attention. Some irregularities, such as very heavy bleeding, missed periods, or severe cramps, may be signs of underlying health conditions that need to be addressed. By tracking their cycles, girls can be more proactive about their health.

Addressing Myths and Misconceptions About Puberty

Puberty is often surrounded by myths and misconceptions, especially regarding sexual health and menstruation. These myths can create confusion, shame, and anxiety among adolescents. For instance, many cultures perpetuate the idea that menstruation is "unclean" or "dirty," leading to feelings of embarrassment or reluctance to discuss it openly. Some may believe that certain foods or activities, such as swimming, should be avoided during menstruation, even though these ideas are not based on scientific evidence.

Another common misconception is that sexual intercourse is the only way to become pregnant. Adolescents should be educated about the different ways pregnancy can occur, including the possibility of becoming pregnant from pre-ejaculate (pre-cum) during unprotected sex. Understanding the risks of unprotected sexual activity and the importance of contraception can help prevent unintended pregnancies and sexually transmitted infections (STIs).

It is also important to address myths about sexual orientation, relationships, and consent. Adolescents should be taught that sexual orientation is a personal aspect of their identity, and it can be fluid and evolving. Additionally, they must understand the concept of consent and the importance of mutual respect in all relationships, whether sexual or otherwise.

The Role of Education and Family in Puberty

While schools play an essential role in educating adolescents about puberty and reproductive health, the family plays a critical part as well. Parents and caregivers are often the first individuals to introduce children to concepts related to their bodies and sexual health. Open communication between parents and children fosters a sense of trust and comfort, making it easier for adolescents to ask questions and seek guidance during puberty.

Parents can help adolescents navigate puberty by providing accurate, age-appropriate information about reproductive health. They should also encourage their children to ask questions and express any concerns they may have. Creating an open environment where discussions about puberty, menstruation, and sexual health are normalized can significantly reduce the stigma surrounding these topics.

In addition to family education, schools should provide comprehensive reproductive health education that includes information about puberty, sexual health, relationships, and contraception. Schools should teach students about the biological, emotional, and social aspects of puberty and provide a safe space for students to ask questions and learn.

Conclusion

Reproductive health and puberty education are fundamental components of adolescent development. Understanding the changes that occur during puberty and learning how to manage reproductive health can empower adolescents to take control of their bodies and make informed decisions about their well-being. By addressing myths, providing accurate information, and fostering open communication between adolescents, families, and educators, we can ensure that adolescents grow up to be healthy, confident, and responsible adults.

Education about menstrual health, hygiene, and reproductive changes is crucial in removing the stigma and confusion that often surround these topics. Adolescents must also be equipped with the knowledge to make safe and healthy choices when it comes to relationships, sexuality, and reproduction. The role of the family and school in providing this education cannot be overstated, as they are key to supporting adolescents during this critical period of growth and self-discovery.

By providing comprehensive, honest, and open discussions about puberty and reproductive health, we can help adolescents navigate these changes with confidence, ultimately contributing to their long-term health and well-being.

CHAPTER IX

SUBSTANCE ABUSE AWARENESS AND PREVENTION

Substance abuse during adolescence is a significant concern for individuals, families, and societies worldwide. The adolescent years are a critical developmental period in which individuals undergo numerous physical, emotional, and psychological changes. These changes can make adolescents more vulnerable to external influences, such as peer pressure and social media, which may contribute to risky behaviours, including substance abuse. Understanding the risks, causes, and preventive measures related to substance use is crucial in ensuring the well-being of adolescents and helping them make healthy, informed decisions.

Substance abuse refers to the harmful or hazardous use of psychoactive substances, including alcohol, tobacco, prescription medications, and illicit drugs. It is important to recognize that substance abuse not only affects physical health but also impairs mental, emotional, and social functioning. Adolescents who engage in substance abuse are at a higher risk of developing long-term health problems, including addiction, impaired cognitive development, mental health disorders, and social difficulties. This chapter explores the risks of substance abuse, the common substances used by adolescents, the factors that influence substance use, and the strategies for prevention and intervention.

Understanding the Risks of Substance Abuse

Substance abuse during adolescence can have long-lasting consequences on an individual's health and overall development. The adolescent brain is still developing, and the use of substances during this critical time can interfere with the natural growth and maturation of brain structures involved in memory, decision-making, and impulse control. Research has shown that the earlier an individual begins using substances, the more likely they are to develop a substance use disorder (SUD) later in life. The following are some of the risks associated with substance abuse in adolescence.

1. Physical Health Consequences

Substance abuse can have a profound impact on an adolescent's physical health. Common substances like alcohol, tobacco, and illicit drugs can damage vital organs, including the liver, lungs, heart, and brain. For instance, smoking cigarettes during adolescence can increase the risk of respiratory diseases, lung cancer, and heart disease later in life. Similarly, excessive alcohol consumption can lead to liver damage, cardiovascular issues, and increased risk of accidents, including motor vehicle crashes.

Additionally, certain illicit drugs, such as marijuana, cocaine, and heroin, can impair cognitive functioning, motor skills, and coordination. The negative effects of substance abuse may hinder an adolescent's ability to perform well in school, engage in physical activities, and maintain relationships with peers and family members.

2. Mental Health Risks

Adolescents who abuse substances are more likely to develop mental health problems, including depression, anxiety, and mood disorders. The chemical changes in the brain caused by substance use can alter mood regulation and exacerbate existing mental health conditions. For example, alcohol and drug use can worsen feelings of depression and anxiety, leading to a cycle of substance abuse as adolescents attempt to self-medicate their emotional distress.

Substance abuse can also impair cognitive functioning, leading to difficulties in concentration, memory, and decision-making. This can affect academic performance and social relationships, contributing to low self-esteem and further mental health challenges.

3. Social and Behavioural Consequences

Substance abuse during adolescence can affect an individual's behaviour and social relationships. Adolescents who use substances are more likely to engage in risky behaviours, such as unprotected sex, driving under the influence, or engaging in criminal activities. Substance use can also lead to problems at school, such as absenteeism, poor grades, and disciplinary issues.

Socially, adolescents who abuse substances may experience strained relationships with family members, friends, and peers. They may face rejection or isolation from their peer groups, leading to feelings of loneliness and alienation. This can further exacerbate mental health problems and contribute to a downward spiral of substance abuse and emotional distress.

Common Substances Abused by Adolescents

Adolescents are exposed to a variety of substances, some legal and some illegal, that can be abused. The substances most commonly abused by adolescents include alcohol, tobacco, marijuana, prescription medications, and illicit drugs. Each of these substances carries its own risks and can lead to a range of harmful consequences when used improperly.

1. Alcohol

Alcohol is the most commonly abused substance among adolescents. Although alcohol is legal for adults in most countries, its use during adolescence can have serious consequences. Adolescents may consume alcohol to fit in with peers, cope with stress, or experiment with their newfound independence. However, alcohol use can impair judgment, coordination, and decision-making, increasing the risk of accidents, injuries, and risky behaviours.

Heavy alcohol use during adolescence is associated with an increased risk of developing alcohol dependence or alcoholism in adulthood. Additionally, alcohol abuse can interfere with brain development, leading to cognitive deficits, poor academic performance, and social difficulties.

2. Tobacco and Nicotine

Tobacco use, particularly smoking cigarettes, remains a major public health concern. Many adolescents are introduced to tobacco use through peer pressure, family influence, or the desire to fit in. Smoking during adolescence can damage the lungs, heart, and circulatory system, leading to long-term health problems such as chronic obstructive pulmonary disease (COPD), lung cancer, and cardiovascular disease.

The use of nicotine products, such as e-cigarettes and vaping devices, has also become increasingly popular among adolescents. While often marketed as a safer alternative to traditional smoking, vaping still exposes the body to harmful chemicals, and the long-term health effects are not yet fully understood.

3. Marijuana

Marijuana is one of the most commonly used illicit drugs among adolescents. Despite its legalization in several countries and states, marijuana use among adolescents can have serious consequences. Marijuana use during adolescence can impair cognitive development, memory, and learning ability. It is also associated with an increased risk of mental health problems, including depression and anxiety.

Adolescents who use marijuana are more likely to engage in risky behaviours, such as driving under the influence or experimenting with other substances. Chronic marijuana use can also lead to dependency and withdrawal symptoms when an individual attempts to stop using the drug.

4. Prescription Medications

Prescription drug abuse has become an alarming trend among adolescents. Commonly abused prescription medications include opioid painkillers (e.g., oxycodone, hydrocodone), stimulants (e.g., Adderall), and benzodiazepines (e.g., Xanax). Adolescents may abuse prescription drugs to achieve a desired effect, such as euphoria, relaxation, or heightened focus. However, the misuse of prescription medications can lead to serious health risks, including overdose, addiction, and even death.

The rise in prescription drug abuse highlights the need for increased awareness and education about the proper use and potential dangers of medications. It is important for adolescents to understand that using prescription drugs without a doctor's guidance can have life-threatening consequences.

5. Illicit Drugs

Illicit drugs such as cocaine, heroin, and methamphetamine are highly addictive and pose severe health risks. These drugs can cause immediate physical harm, including respiratory depression, heart attack, and overdose. Chronic use of illicit drugs can lead to long-term health problems, including organ damage, cognitive decline, and mental health disorders.

The use of illicit drugs is often linked to social and environmental factors, such as peer pressure, poverty, and trauma. Adolescents who abuse these drugs are at a higher risk of engaging in criminal behaviour, facing legal consequences, and experiencing long-term social and psychological difficulties.

Factors Contributing to Adolescent Substance Abuse

Substance abuse is influenced by a combination of biological, psychological, social, and environmental factors. Understanding these factors can help identify adolescents who may be at risk of substance abuse and guide prevention efforts.

1. Peer Pressure

Peer pressure is one of the most significant factors influencing adolescent substance use. Adolescents often face pressure from their friends and peers to conform to certain behaviours, including drinking alcohol or using drugs. The desire for social acceptance and fear of rejection can drive adolescents to engage in risky behaviours, even if they are aware of the potential consequences.

2. Family Dynamics

Family relationships and dynamics play a crucial role in adolescent behaviour. Adolescents who come from families with a history of substance abuse or dysfunctional relationships may be more likely to experiment with drugs or alcohol. Poor communication, neglect, or abuse can contribute to emotional distress, leading adolescents to turn to substances as a coping mechanism.

3. Mental Health Disorders

Adolescents with mental health disorders, such as depression, anxiety, or ADHD, are at a higher risk of substance abuse. Substance use may be seen as a way to self-medicate and cope with emotional pain. However, substance abuse often exacerbates mental health issues, creating a vicious cycle of addiction and distress.

4. Social and Environmental Factors

The social environment, including school, community, and cultural norms, can influence substance use among adolescents. For example, adolescents who attend schools or live in communities where substance use is prevalent may be more likely to experiment with drugs or alcohol. Similarly, exposure to media that glamorizes substance use can normalize risky behaviour and encourage experimentation.

Prevention Strategies for Substance Abuse

Preventing substance abuse in adolescents requires a multifaceted approach that involves education, intervention, and support from families, schools, and communities. Below are some effective strategies for preventing adolescent substance abuse:

1. Education and Awareness

Education is one of the most effective tools in preventing substance abuse. Adolescents need to understand the risks and consequences of using substances, both in the short and long term. Comprehensive drug education programs should be implemented in schools to teach adolescents about the dangers of substance abuse, how to resist peer pressure, and how to make healthy choices.

2. Building Strong Family Relationships

Families play a central role in preventing substance abuse. Open communication, positive role models, and emotional support can help adolescents resist the temptation to experiment with substances. Families should establish clear boundaries, expectations, and consequences regarding substance use. Engaging in family activities and spending quality time together can also strengthen family bonds and reduce the likelihood of substance abuse.

3. Promoting Healthy Coping Skills

Adolescents need to develop healthy coping mechanisms to manage stress, anxiety, and emotional distress. Encouraging activities such as sports, art, music, or meditation can provide adolescents with positive outlets for emotional expression. Teaching stress management techniques and promoting resilience can help adolescents navigate the challenges of adolescence without resorting to substance use.

4. Peer Support Programs

Peer support programs can be an effective way to prevent substance abuse. These programs provide adolescents with the opportunity to connect with peers who share similar values and experiences. Peer mentors can offer guidance, support, and encouragement to resist peer pressure and make healthy choices.

5. Early Intervention and Counselling

Early intervention is critical in addressing substance abuse before it becomes a long-term problem. Adolescents who show signs of substance abuse should be provided with counselling and support services. Counselling can help adolescents address underlying emotional or psychological issues that may contribute to substance use. In some cases, treatment programs or rehabilitation may be necessary to help adolescents recover from addiction.

Conclusion

Substance abuse is a serious issue that can have long-lasting consequences on the health and development of adolescents. Understanding the risks of substance abuse, the common substances abused by adolescents, and the factors that contribute to substance use is crucial in developing effective prevention and intervention strategies. Families, schools, and communities must work together to provide adolescents with the education, support, and resources they need to make healthy, informed choices. By fostering open communication, building strong relationships, and promoting healthy coping skills, we can help adolescents navigate the challenges of adolescence and reduce the risk of substance abuse.

CHAPTER X

EMPOWERING ADOLESCENTS FOR LIFELONG HEALTH

Adolescence is a period of significant growth, transition, and change. During these formative years, individuals develop physical, emotional, and psychological characteristics that will shape their lives well into adulthood. The choices and habits that adolescents form during this time can have a lasting impact on their health, well-being, and overall quality of life. Thus, it is essential to equip adolescents with the knowledge, skills, and resources needed to empower them to adopt healthy habits, make informed decisions, and build a foundation for lifelong health.

This chapter aims to provide a comprehensive overview of the various factors that contribute to adolescent health, the importance of developing healthy habits, and strategies for empowering adolescents to take control of their health. The focus will be on the key components of physical health, nutrition, mental well-being, and the development of positive life skills, all of which contribute to a balanced and fulfilling life. The chapter will also explore the role of healthcare professionals, schools, and families in supporting adolescents as they navigate this critical stage of development and prepare for the challenges and opportunities of adulthood.

The Importance of Lifelong Health

Lifelong health refers to the sustained well-being of an individual throughout their life, with an emphasis on the prevention of chronic diseases, the promotion of mental health, and the maintenance of physical and emotional fitness. Establishing healthy habits during adolescence is key to ensuring long-term health. Research shows that behaviours adopted during adolescence, such as exercise, eating habits, sleep patterns, and substance use, often persist into adulthood. For example, adolescents who engage in regular physical activity are more likely to remain active in adulthood, leading to improved cardiovascular health, lower rates of obesity, and reduced risk of chronic diseases such as diabetes and hypertension.

Additionally, mental health is an integral component of lifelong health. Adolescents are particularly vulnerable to mental health challenges due to the complex changes they experience, including hormonal fluctuations, developing self-identity, peer relationships, academic pressures, and the increasing influence of social media. By fostering resilience and emotional regulation during adolescence, individuals can better cope with stress, anxiety, and challenges throughout their lives, promoting mental and emotional well-being in adulthood.

Ultimately, empowering adolescents to prioritize their health can help them lead productive, fulfilling lives, prevent early onset of chronic diseases, reduce health inequalities, and contribute positively to society. This chapter will focus on empowering adolescents in the following key areas: physical health, mental well-being, decision-making, goal-setting, and personal responsibility.

Physical Health: Establishing Healthy Habits

Adolescence is a time when individuals experience rapid physical growth and development. It is also a time when they begin to gain greater independence and autonomy, including making decisions about their health and lifestyle. Establishing healthy habits during this period is essential for promoting overall physical health and preventing long-term health problems. The foundation for lifelong health is built on practices such as regular physical activity, balanced nutrition, adequate sleep, and regular medical check-ups.

1. Physical Activity and Exercise

Regular physical activity is one of the most important factors for maintaining lifelong health. During adolescence, the body undergoes rapid changes that require physical activity to support growth, strengthen muscles and bones, and promote cardiovascular health. Unfortunately, many adolescents do not engage in enough physical activity, which can contribute to weight gain, obesity, and the development of chronic diseases such as heart disease and diabetes.

Encouraging adolescents to participate in at least 60 minutes of moderate to vigorous physical activity each day can have numerous benefits, including improved muscle strength, bone density, flexibility, and cardiovascular fitness. Physical activity also improves mood, reduces stress, and enhances cognitive function, contributing to better academic performance and mental well-being.

Adolescents can engage in physical activities such as running, swimming, cycling, dancing, playing sports, or even participating in activities like yoga or hiking. It is important for adolescents to find physical activities they enjoy, as this will increase the likelihood of long-term engagement in an active lifestyle.

2. Nutrition and Healthy Eating

Proper nutrition is essential for the growth and development of adolescents. During this stage of life, adolescents require higher amounts of nutrients, including vitamins, minerals, proteins, and healthy fats, to support their growing bodies and maintain energy levels. Unfortunately, many adolescents consume unhealthy diets that are high in processed foods, sugars, and unhealthy fats, leading to poor nutrition and weight gain.

Adolescents should be educated on the importance of a balanced diet that includes a variety of nutrient-dense foods. A healthy eating plan should consist of:

- **Fruits and Vegetables**: Rich in vitamins, minerals, and antioxidants that promote overall health.
- **Whole Grains**: Provide fibre and essential nutrients that aid digestion and regulate blood sugar levels.
- **Lean Proteins**: Sources like chicken, fish, beans, and nuts support muscle growth and tissue repair.
- **Healthy Fats**: Unsaturated fats from sources like avocados, olive oil, and nuts support brain function and hormone regulation.
- **Dairy or Dairy Alternatives**: Provide calcium for bone health and support muscle function.

In addition to emphasizing the importance of healthy foods, adolescents should also be educated on portion control, hydration, and the dangers of overconsumption of unhealthy foods, such as sugary snacks, fast food, and sugary drinks. Encouraging the consumption of water and minimizing the intake of sugary beverages is vital for preventing obesity and maintaining healthy hydration levels.

3. Sleep Hygiene

Adequate sleep is crucial for adolescent health. Sleep supports physical growth, cognitive function, and emotional well-being. However, many adolescents struggle with sleep deprivation due to increased academic pressures, extracurricular activities, social media use, and irregular sleep schedules.

Sleep deprivation can negatively impact cognitive function, memory retention, mood regulation, and academic performance. Chronic sleep deprivation is also associated with an increased risk of obesity, mental health disorders, and substance abuse. Adolescents should aim to get 8–10 hours of sleep each night to support their physical and mental health.

Promoting good sleep hygiene, such as maintaining a consistent sleep schedule, creating a relaxing bedtime routine, and limiting screen time before bed, can help improve sleep quality and duration.

4. Preventive Healthcare and Regular Check-ups

Routine healthcare visits are essential for maintaining adolescent health and preventing potential health problems. Adolescents should undergo regular check-ups with their primary care provider, including vaccinations, screenings, and preventive counselling. These visits offer an opportunity for healthcare professionals to monitor physical growth, identify early signs of health problems, and provide guidance on healthy habits.

Additionally, healthcare professionals should provide education on topics such as sexual and reproductive health, mental health, and substance abuse prevention, ensuring that adolescents receive accurate and age-appropriate information about their health.

Mental Well-being: Building Resilience and Emotional Intelligence

Adolescence is a time of significant emotional development, and mental health plays a pivotal role in overall well-being. Adolescents face many challenges during this period, including academic pressures, changing social dynamics, and the exploration of their identity. These challenges, combined with the hormonal changes occurring during adolescence, can contribute to stress, anxiety, depression, and emotional instability.

Empowering adolescents to develop emotional resilience, emotional intelligence, and healthy coping mechanisms can help them navigate these challenges and build a strong foundation for mental well-being throughout their lives. Adolescents who develop emotional intelligence are better able to understand and manage their emotions, build positive relationships, and cope with stress effectively.

1. Understanding Mental Health

Mental health encompasses emotional, psychological, and social well-being. It affects how individuals think, feel, and behave. During adolescence, the brain undergoes significant changes that influence emotional regulation, decision-making, and self-perception. As such, mental health during adolescence is often marked by heightened sensitivity to stress, anxiety, and mood fluctuations.

Education about mental health is crucial for helping adolescents understand the importance of emotional well-being and the signs and symptoms of common mental health conditions, such as depression, anxiety, and eating disorders. Adolescents should also be encouraged to seek help when they experience emotional distress, as early intervention can prevent the development of more severe mental health issues.

2. Building Emotional Resilience

Emotional resilience refers to the ability to adapt to and recover from adversity, stress, and challenges. Adolescents who develop resilience are better equipped to cope with the ups and downs of life, including academic pressures, peer relationships, and family issues.

Building resilience involves teaching adolescents' skills such as problem-solving, goal-setting, self-reflection, and stress management. Encouraging healthy coping strategies, such as mindfulness, journaling, physical activity, and talking to trusted adults, can help adolescents manage difficult emotions and stay grounded during stressful times.

3. Fostering Positive Relationships and Social Support

Strong social connections are essential for mental well-being. Adolescents benefit from having a network of supportive family members, friends, mentors, and peers who provide emotional support, guidance, and encouragement. Positive relationships help adolescents build self-esteem, gain a sense of belonging, and develop important social skills.

Parents, caregivers, and educators should work to create a supportive environment for adolescents, where open communication, trust, and empathy are valued. Encouraging adolescents to seek out friendships with individuals who share similar values and interests can help them build healthy, positive relationships.

Developing Life Skills: Decision-making, Goal-setting, and Personal Responsibility

Empowering adolescents to take responsibility for their health and well-being involves fostering key life skills that promote self-sufficiency, independence, and self-awareness. These skills are crucial for making informed decisions, setting realistic goals, and achieving long-term success in various areas of life, including education, career, relationships, and personal growth.

1. Decision-making Skills

Decision-making is an essential skill that adolescents need to develop as they transition to adulthood. Adolescents are constantly faced with decisions, whether related to academics, social situations, or their personal lives. Teaching adolescents how to make informed, thoughtful decisions can help them navigate challenges and avoid risky behaviours, such as substance abuse, unsafe sexual practices, and academic underachievement.

A key aspect of decision-making is understanding the potential consequences of one's actions. Adolescents should be encouraged to think critically about the choices they make and consider both the short-term and long-term impacts on their health and well-being.

2. Goal-setting and Planning for the Future

Goal-setting is a powerful tool for achieving personal success and growth. Adolescents should be encouraged to set both short-term and long-term goals that align with their values and aspirations. Whether these goals are related to academic performance, career aspirations, health, or personal development, having clear goals provides adolescents with a sense of purpose and direction.

Teaching adolescents how to set SMART goals (Specific, Measurable, Achievable, Relevant, and Time-bound) can help them break down larger goals into manageable steps. Additionally, goal-setting fosters a sense of accomplishment and boosts self-confidence as adolescents work toward their objectives.

3. Taking Personal Responsibility

Adolescence is a time when individuals begin to take on greater responsibility for their lives. This includes taking responsibility for their health, decisions, actions, and relationships. By encouraging adolescents to take ownership of their choices and outcomes, they can develop a sense of accountability and learn to navigate the challenges of adulthood with confidence.

Parents, educators, and healthcare professionals play a crucial role in supporting adolescents in this process by providing guidance, setting clear expectations, and offering positive reinforcement for responsible behaviour.

Conclusion

Empowering adolescents for lifelong health require a multifaceted approach that emphasizes physical health, mental well-being, decision-making, and personal responsibility. By providing adolescents with the knowledge, tools, and resources they need to make informed choices, we can help them develop the skills necessary to thrive throughout their lives.

Healthcare professionals, educators, parents, and communities all have an essential role to play in supporting adolescents during this critical period of development. Through a combination of education, guidance, and empowerment, we can help adolescents create a solid foundation for lifelong health and well-being, equipping them to face the challenges of adulthood with resilience and confidence.

CHAPTER XI

NUTRITION AND HEALTHY EATING HABITS

Nutrition plays a crucial role in adolescent growth, development, and overall well-being. The teenage years are a period of rapid physical, cognitive, and emotional changes, making it essential to consume a balanced diet that meets increased energy and nutrient demands. Good nutrition fosters healthy brain development, supports a strong immune system, and helps maintain an optimal body weight. However, many adolescents struggle with unhealthy eating habits, driven by peer pressure, social media influences, and busy schedules. Understanding the fundamentals of nutrition and making informed dietary choices can promote long-term health and prevent chronic diseases.

This chapter explores the importance of proper nutrition, the components of a balanced diet, common nutritional deficiencies in teenagers, practical strategies for healthy eating, and tips for overcoming dietary challenges.

The Importance of Good Nutrition in Adolescence

1. Physical Growth and Development

During adolescence, the body undergoes significant changes, including rapid growth spurts, hormonal shifts, and increased muscle and bone development. Proper nutrition provides the necessary fuel for these changes. Key nutrients such as protein, calcium, iron, and essential vitamins play a fundamental role in supporting bone health, muscle function, and overall physical development.

2. Brain Health and Cognitive Function

Nutrient-rich foods, including omega-3 fatty acids, B vitamins, and antioxidants, enhance cognitive function, memory, and concentration. These nutrients support brain development and help adolescents stay focused in school, retain information, and improve problem-solving skills. On the other hand, excessive consumption of processed and sugary foods has been linked to reduced cognitive function and mental fatigue.

3. Mental Health and Emotional Well-Being

Research shows that diet has a direct impact on mental health. A well-balanced diet can help regulate mood, reduce anxiety and depression, and boost overall emotional resilience. Nutrient-rich foods, such as whole grains, lean proteins, and leafy greens, support neurotransmitter production, which influences feelings of happiness and stress management.

4. Preventing Chronic Diseases

Poor dietary choices can contribute to long-term health issues, such as obesity, type 2 diabetes, heart disease, and osteoporosis. Developing healthy eating habits in adolescence significantly reduces the risk of these conditions later in life. Eating a variety of nutrient-dense foods while limiting processed and high-sugar options can set a strong foundation for lifelong well-being.

Components of a Balanced Diet

A well-balanced diet includes a combination of macronutrients (proteins, carbohydrates, and fats) and micronutrients (vitamins and minerals). Each plays a unique role in maintaining optimal health.

1. Macronutrients

- **Proteins**: Essential for muscle growth, tissue repair, and immune function. Sources include lean meats, poultry, fish, eggs, beans, lentils, and dairy products.
- **Carbohydrates**: Provide energy for daily activities and brain function. Healthy sources include whole grains, fruits, vegetables, and legumes.
- **Fats**: Support brain development and hormone production. Healthy fats include avocados, nuts, seeds, olive oil, and fatty fish.

2. Micronutrients

- **Calcium**: Vital for bone health and strength. Found in dairy products, leafy greens, and fortified plant-based alternatives.
- **Iron**: Crucial for oxygen transport and energy production. Found in lean meats, beans, spinach, and fortified cereals.
- **Vitamins and Minerals**: Support immune function, skin health, and overall body processes. Key sources include fruits, vegetables, nuts, and whole grains.

Common Nutritional Deficiencies in Adolescents

Many teenagers experience nutrient deficiencies due to unhealthy dietary choices, lack of knowledge, or restrictive eating habits. The most common deficiencies include:

- **Iron Deficiency**: Can lead to anaemia, fatigue, and decreased concentration.
- **Calcium Deficiency**: Increases the risk of weak bones and osteoporosis in later years.
- **Vitamin D Deficiency**: Affects bone health and immune function.
- **Fibre Deficiency**: Leads to digestive issues and increased risk of obesity.
- **Protein Deficiency**: May result in poor muscle development and a weakened immune system.

To prevent these deficiencies, adolescents should focus on consuming a diverse and balanced diet that includes a variety of nutrient-dense foods.

Strategies for Healthy Eating

Adopting healthy eating habits can be challenging, especially with the abundance of processed foods and fast-food options. However, implementing small, sustainable changes can lead to lasting improvements in overall nutrition.

1. Planning Balanced Meals

- Incorporate a variety of food groups into each meal to ensure adequate nutrient intake.
- Aim for half a plate of vegetables, a quarter plate of protein, and a quarter plate of whole grains.
- Choose whole, unprocessed foods over refined and fast-food options.

2. Making Healthy Snack Choices

- Replace chips and sugary snacks with nuts, fruits, yogurt, or hummus with vegetables.
- Keep healthy snacks readily available to reduce the temptation for junk food.
- Avoid excessive consumption of sugary drinks and opt for water, herbal teas, or natural fruit juices.

3. Understanding Food Labels

- Learn to read ingredient lists and nutrition facts to make informed choices.
- Avoid foods high in added sugars, unhealthy fats, and artificial preservatives.
- Choose products labelled as whole grain, low sugar, and rich in fibre.

4. Practicing Mindful Eating

- Eat slowly and pay attention to hunger and fullness cues.

- Avoid distractions like TV or smartphones while eating.
- Focus on enjoying the flavours and textures of food.

5. Staying Hydrated

- Drink at least 8 cups (2 litres) of water daily to support metabolism and digestion.
- Limit sugary drinks like sodas and energy drinks, which can lead to weight gain and energy crashes.
- Herbal teas and infused water are great alternatives to plain water.
-

Overcoming Dietary Challenges

Many adolescents face challenges when trying to maintain a healthy diet. These include time constraints, peer pressure, and lack of access to nutritious food. Here are some strategies to overcome common obstacles:

- **Busy Schedules**: Prepare meals and snacks in advance to avoid relying on fast food.
- **Peer Influence**: Educate friends about the benefits of healthy eating and make mindful choices together.
- **Budget-Friendly Eating**: Buy whole foods in bulk, choose seasonal produce, and cook at home to save money.
- **Cultural and Dietary Restrictions**: Explore nutritious options that align with personal dietary preferences and cultural practices.

Conclusion

Healthy nutrition is a cornerstone of adolescent well-being, influencing physical growth, mental health, and disease prevention. By consuming a balanced diet rich in proteins, healthy fats, whole grains, fruits, and vegetables, teenagers can build strong foundations for a healthy future. Adopting mindful eating habits, making informed food choices, and overcoming dietary challenges will set the stage for lifelong wellness. Encouraging nutrition education and making small, positive changes can have a profound impact on an adolescent's health and overall quality of life.

CHAPTER XII

PHYSICAL ACTIVITIES AND FITNESS

Introduction

Physical activity and fitness are essential components of a healthy lifestyle, particularly during adolescence. This stage of life is characterized by rapid growth, increased energy demands, and evolving lifestyle habits that can have long-term effects on health. Engaging in regular physical activity not only enhances physical health but also improves mental well-being, boosts academic performance, and fosters social connections. However, modern lifestyles, technological advancements, and sedentary habits have made it increasingly difficult for many teenagers to maintain an active routine.

This chapter explores the importance of physical activity, different types of exercises, benefits of an active lifestyle, barriers to fitness, and strategies for incorporating movement into daily life.

The Importance of Physical Activity in Adolescence

1. Physical Growth and Development

During adolescence, the body undergoes significant physiological changes, including muscle growth, bone development, and hormonal shifts. Regular physical activity supports these changes by enhancing cardiovascular health, improving muscle strength, and boosting endurance.

2. Mental and Emotional Well-being

Exercise has a profound impact on mental health. Physical activity stimulates the release of endorphins—hormones that promote feelings of happiness and reduce stress. Regular movement can help alleviate symptoms of anxiety and depression, improve self-esteem, and enhance overall emotional resilience.

3. Academic and Cognitive Benefits

Research suggests that students who engage in regular physical activity perform better academically. Exercise increases blood flow to the brain, improves concentration, and enhances memory retention, leading to improved problem-solving skills and greater academic success.

4. Prevention of Chronic Diseases

Engaging in regular exercise reduces the risk of obesity, type 2 diabetes, heart disease, and osteoporosis. Establishing active habits during adolescence can prevent the onset of chronic illnesses in adulthood.

Types of Physical Activity

To achieve well-rounded fitness, adolescents should incorporate various types of exercises into their routine:

1. Aerobic Exercises

Aerobic activities, also known as cardio, improve heart and lung health. Examples include:

- Running
- Swimming
- Cycling
- Dancing
- Jump rope

2. Strength Training

Strength exercises help build muscle mass, enhance endurance, and improve metabolism. Examples include:

- Bodyweight exercises (push-ups, squats, lunges)
- Weightlifting
- Resistance band training
- Functional training

3. Flexibility and Mobility Workouts

Flexibility exercises enhance range of motion, reduce injury risk, and improve posture. Examples include:

- Yoga
- Stretching routines
- Pilates
- Dynamic mobility drills

4. Recreational and Team Sports

Sports provide social interaction, teamwork skills, and a fun way to stay active. Popular sports include:

- Soccer
- Basketball
- Tennis
- Volleyball
- Martial arts

Recommended Physical Activity Guidelines

Health experts recommend the following activity levels for adolescents:

- At least 60 minutes of moderate-to-vigorous physical activity daily.

- Muscle-strengthening and bone-strengthening exercises at least three days per week.
- Regular movement throughout the day to avoid prolonged sedentary behaviour.

Barriers to Physical Activity

Despite the known benefits, many adolescents struggle to maintain an active lifestyle due to several barriers:

1. Screen Time and Technology

Excessive time spent on social media, video games, and television contributes to sedentary behaviour and decreased activity levels.

2. Busy Academic and Social Schedules

Homework, school responsibilities, and extracurricular commitments can make it difficult to prioritize exercise.

3. Lack of Access to Facilities

Not all teens have access to gyms, sports fields, or safe outdoor spaces for exercise.

4. Low Motivation and Peer Influence

Some adolescents lack motivation or feel discouraged by negative peer comparisons, leading to inactivity.

Strategies for Incorporating Exercise into Daily Life

To overcome barriers and maintain an active lifestyle, adolescents can adopt the following strategies:

1. Find Enjoyable Activities

Not everyone enjoys the same type of exercise. Experiment with different activities to find something engaging, whether it's dancing, hiking, or martial arts.

2. Set Realistic Fitness Goals

Start with small, achievable goals and gradually increase intensity. Examples include:

- Walking 10,000 steps daily
- Completing a 30-minute workout three times a week
- Learning a new sport or physical skill

3. Incorporate Movement into Daily Routine

- Take the stairs instead of the elevator
- Walk or cycle to school
- Stretch or do short exercises during study breaks

4. Join a Sports Team or Group

Participating in group activities can make exercise more enjoyable and increase accountability.

5. Reduce Sedentary Time

- Set screen time limits
- Use apps that remind you to take movement breaks
- Engage in active hobbies like gardening or dancing

The Role of Nutrition in Fitness

Exercise and nutrition go hand in hand. Proper fueling is necessary to support physical activity and recovery. Key nutritional guidelines include:

- Eating a balanced diet with adequate protein, carbohydrates, and healthy fats
- Staying hydrated by drinking plenty of water before, during, and after exercise
- Avoiding excessive consumption of processed foods and sugary drinks
- Consuming post-workout meals rich in protein to aid muscle recovery

The Connection Between Sleep and Fitness

Adequate sleep is crucial for recovery and performance. Lack of sleep can lead to decreased motivation, poor muscle repair, and increased injury risk. Adolescents should aim for 8-10 hours of sleep per night to optimize fitness and overall well-being.

Monitoring Progress and Staying Motivated

Tracking fitness progress can help maintain motivation and encourage consistency. Methods for tracking include:

- Keeping a workout journal
- Using fitness apps or wearable trackers
- Setting short-term and long-term fitness milestones

Celebrating small achievements and staying patient with progress is key to sustaining an active lifestyle.

Conclusion

Physical activity and fitness are integral to adolescent health and well-being. Engaging in regular exercise enhances physical growth, mental health, and academic performance while reducing the risk of chronic diseases. By overcoming common barriers, setting realistic goals, and incorporating movement into daily life, adolescents can build a strong foundation for a lifelong active lifestyle. Prioritizing exercise, maintaining a balanced diet, and ensuring proper rest will lead to a healthier and more fulfilling life.

CHAPTER XIII

SLEEP HYGIENE AND ITS IMPORTANCE

Introduction

Sleep plays a crucial role in adolescent development, influencing cognitive function, emotional stability, and physical health. Despite its importance, many teenagers do not get adequate sleep due to academic pressure, social engagements, and increased screen time. Poor sleep hygiene can lead to a variety of health issues, including fatigue, weakened immune function, poor academic performance, and heightened stress levels. Understanding the principles of good sleep hygiene and implementing effective strategies can improve sleep quality and overall well-being.

This chapter explores the significance of sleep, the consequences of poor sleep habits, factors affecting sleep quality, and practical strategies to enhance sleep hygiene.

The Importance of Sleep in Adolescence

1. Cognitive Function and Academic Performance

Sleep is essential for memory consolidation, learning, and problem-solving skills. Research has shown that students who get adequate sleep perform better in school, exhibit greater focus, and retain information more effectively. Sleep deprivation, on the other hand, leads to reduced attention span, impaired judgment, and decreased academic success.

2. Emotional and Mental Health

Adolescents with poor sleep patterns are more likely to experience mood swings, anxiety, and depression. Sleep helps regulate emotional responses, making it easier to manage stress and maintain positive social interactions. Chronic sleep deprivation has been linked to increased irritability, impulsivity, and difficulty coping with daily challenges.

3. Physical Health and Growth

During sleep, the body undergoes crucial repair processes. Growth hormone is released during deep sleep, aiding in physical development, muscle repair, and immune system strengthening. Insufficient sleep can disrupt these processes, leading to stunted growth, increased susceptibility to illnesses, and metabolic imbalances.

4. Energy Levels and Productivity

A well-rested individual has higher energy levels and better stamina throughout the day. Poor sleep contributes to fatigue, sluggishness, and decreased motivation, affecting both academic and extracurricular activities.

Consequences of Poor Sleep Hygiene

Failure to establish good sleep habits can lead to various negative effects:

- **Increased Risk of Obesity**: Lack of sleep disrupts hunger-regulating hormones, leading to overeating and weight gain.
- **Weakened Immune System**: Poor sleep reduces the body's ability to fight infections and recover from illnesses.
- **Increased Risk of Accidents**: Sleep deprivation impairs reaction time, increasing the likelihood of accidents and injuries.

- **Difficulty in Emotional Regulation**: Sleep-deprived individuals are more prone to mood disorders, anger, and anxiety.
- **Lower Academic Performance**: Reduced concentration and memory retention negatively impact school performance.

Factors Affecting Sleep Quality

Several factors can influence the quality and duration of sleep:

1. Screen Time and Blue Light Exposure

The use of electronic devices before bedtime exposes the brain to blue light, which suppresses the production of melatonin, the sleep hormone. This makes it harder to fall asleep and reduces overall sleep quality.

2. Irregular Sleep Schedules

Many adolescents go to bed at different times throughout the week, disrupting their internal biological clock. Irregular sleep patterns make it harder to establish a consistent sleep routine, leading to sleep deprivation.

3. Caffeine and Stimulant Consumption

Drinks like coffee, energy drinks, and sodas contain caffeine, a stimulant that keeps the brain alert and delays sleep onset. Consuming these beverages in the evening can significantly impact sleep quality.

4. Stress and Anxiety

Academic pressure, social expectations, and personal challenges can contribute to high stress levels, making it difficult to relax before bedtime. Racing thoughts and worry can interfere with the ability to fall and stay asleep.

5. Sleep Environment

A comfortable sleep environment is essential for restful sleep. Factors such as room temperature, lighting, noise levels, and mattress quality all play a role in sleep hygiene.

Strategies for Improving Sleep Hygiene

To develop healthy sleep habits, adolescents can implement the following strategies:

1. Establish a Consistent Sleep Routine

- Go to bed and wake up at the same time every day, even on weekends.
- Develop a relaxing bedtime routine to signal to the body that it is time to sleep.
- Avoid late-night naps, which can interfere with night-time sleep.

2. Limit Screen Time Before Bed

- Turn off electronic devices at least one hour before bedtime.
- Use blue light filters on screens if usage is unavoidable.
- Engage in screen-free activities such as reading, journaling, or listening to calming music.

3. Create a Comfortable Sleep Environment

- Keep the bedroom cool, dark, and quiet.
- Use blackout curtains or an eye mask to block out light.
- Invest in a comfortable mattress and pillows to enhance sleep quality.

4. Manage Stress and Anxiety

- Practice relaxation techniques such as deep breathing, meditation, or yoga before bed.
- Write down worries in a journal to clear the mind before sleeping.
- Engage in physical activity during the day to reduce stress levels.

5. Monitor Diet and Hydration

- Avoid heavy meals, caffeine, and sugary snacks before bedtime.
- Drink enough water throughout the day but limit fluid intake close to bedtime to reduce night-time awakenings.

The Role of Naps in Sleep Hygiene

Short naps can be beneficial, but excessive or poorly timed naps can disrupt nighttime sleep. Adolescents should:

- Limit naps to 20-30 minutes to avoid grogginess.
- Take naps earlier in the afternoon rather than close to bedtime.
- Use naps strategically to boost alertness when feeling fatigued.

Tracking Sleep Patterns

Monitoring sleep habits can help identify areas for improvement. Adolescents can use:

- Sleep journals to record bedtime, wake-up time, and overall sleep quality.
- Sleep tracking apps or wearable devices to analyse sleep duration and patterns.

- Feedback from family members on snoring, restlessness, or signs of poor sleep.

Conclusion

Sleep hygiene is a critical component of adolescent health, influencing cognitive function, emotional well-being, and physical development. Establishing a consistent sleep schedule, creating a comfortable sleep environment, managing stress, and limiting screen time can significantly improve sleep quality. By prioritizing good sleep habits, adolescents can enhance their academic performance, emotional resilience, and overall health, setting the foundation for lifelong well-being.

CHAPTER XIV

MANAGING STRESS AND ANXIETY

Introduction

Stress and anxiety are common experiences during adolescence, a time of rapid changes, academic pressures, social expectations, and personal development. While some stress is normal and even beneficial in moderation, excessive or unmanaged stress can negatively impact mental and physical health. Understanding how to recognize stressors, implement coping strategies, and develop resilience can empower adolescents to navigate these challenges effectively.

This chapter explores the causes of stress and anxiety, their effects on mental and physical health, and practical strategies for managing and reducing stress.

Understanding Stress and Anxiety

1. What is Stress?

Stress is the body's response to any demand or challenge. It can be triggered by academic workload, social interactions, family expectations, or personal insecurities. Stress manifests in various ways, including physical tension, emotional irritability, and cognitive overwhelm.

2. What is Anxiety?

Anxiety is a heightened form of stress that involves excessive worry, fear, or nervousness about future events. Unlike short-term stress, anxiety can persist even in the absence of immediate stressors and can interfere with daily life and well-being.

3. Common Causes of Stress and Anxiety in Adolescents

- Academic Pressure: Exams, assignments, and expectations to perform well.
- Social Challenges: Peer pressure, bullying, relationships, and fitting in.
- Family Expectations: Parental pressure to excel in academics or extracurricular activities.
- Body Image Issues: Concerns about physical appearance influenced by social media and societal standards.
- Future Uncertainty: Fear of career choices, college admissions, and life after school.

Effects of Stress and Anxiety on Adolescents

1. Physical Health Impacts

- Headaches, stomach aches, and muscle tension.
- Weakened immune system leading to frequent illnesses.
- Fatigue and sleep disturbances such as insomnia.

2. Emotional and Mental Health Effects

- Increased irritability, mood swings, and emotional outbursts.
- Feelings of hopelessness or depression.
- Difficulty concentrating and decision-making.

3. Behavioural Changes

- Withdrawal from friends and family.

- Engaging in unhealthy coping mechanisms such as overeating or avoiding responsibilities.
- Increased reliance on digital distractions, such as excessive social media use.

Strategies for Managing Stress and Anxiety

1. Recognizing and Identifying Stressors

The first step in managing stress is self-awareness. Adolescents should:

- Maintain a journal to track stressful situations and their responses.
- Reflect on emotional triggers and reactions to different stressors.
- Differentiate between controllable and uncontrollable stressors.

2. Developing Healthy Coping Mechanisms

- Exercise Regularly: Engaging in physical activity such as jogging, yoga, or sports releases endorphins, reducing stress levels.
- Practice Deep Breathing: Controlled breathing techniques help regulate the nervous system and promote relaxation.
- Engage in Creative Activities: Drawing, writing, playing music, or crafting can be effective stress relievers.
- Limit Screen Time: Reducing social media usage can decrease comparison-induced anxiety.
- Prioritize Sleep: Ensuring 8-10 hours of sleep enhances cognitive function and emotional regulation.

3. Time Management and Organization

Proper time management reduces stress associated with deadlines and overwhelming responsibilities:

- Use a Planner: Scheduling tasks and assignments can prevent last-minute panic.
- Break Tasks into Smaller Steps: Completing tasks in segments makes them more manageable.
- Avoid Procrastination: Tackling work early reduces pressure and improves efficiency.

4. Building a Support System

Having a reliable support network is essential in managing stress:

- Talk to Family and Friends: Sharing concerns with trusted individuals provides emotional relief.
- Seek Professional Guidance: Counsellors or therapists can offer valuable strategies for coping with anxiety.
- Join Support Groups: Engaging with others experiencing similar struggles fosters understanding and shared solutions.

5. Practicing Mindfulness and Relaxation Techniques

- Meditation and Mindfulness: Techniques like guided meditation or body scans help centre thoughts and reduce worry.
- Progressive Muscle Relaxation: Tensing and releasing muscles in a systematic way alleviates physical tension.
- Listening to Calming Music: Slow, soothing music can lower heart rate and induce a sense of calmness.

6. Adopting a Positive Mindset

- Reframe Negative Thoughts: Transforming "I can't do this" into "I will do my best" shifts perspective.
- Practice Gratitude: Keeping a gratitude journal improves overall happiness and stress resilience.
- Focus on Self-Compassion: Being kind to oneself prevents unnecessary self-criticism.

When to Seek Professional Help

If stress or anxiety becomes overwhelming and interferes with daily life, professional intervention may be necessary. Warning signs include:

- Persistent sadness or feelings of hopelessness.
- Panic attacks or excessive fears that hinder routine activities.
- Sudden changes in eating or sleeping habits.
- Decline in academic performance or withdrawal from social interactions.
- Engaging in self-harm or expressing thoughts of self-harm.

Therapists, school counsellors, and mental health professionals can provide tailored strategies and support for managing anxiety effectively.

Conclusion

Managing stress and anxiety is crucial for adolescent well-being. Understanding stressors, developing coping mechanisms, and building strong support networks help navigate life's challenges. By adopting relaxation techniques, positive thinking, and time management skills, adolescents can cultivate resilience and maintain emotional balance. Seeking professional help when needed ensures that stress does not become overwhelming, promoting a healthier, happier future.

CHAPTER XV

BUILDING SELF–ESTEEM AND CONFIDENCE

Introduction

Self-esteem and confidence play a crucial role in adolescent development, shaping the way individuals perceive themselves, interact with others, and navigate challenges. Adolescence is a time of self-discovery and identity formation, during which self-esteem can fluctuate based on social experiences, academic performance, personal achievements, and body image concerns. Developing strong self-esteem and confidence fosters resilience, motivation, and a positive outlook on life.

This chapter explores the concept of self-esteem, its impact on adolescent well-being, factors influencing confidence levels, and strategies for cultivating a healthy self-image.

Understanding Self-Esteem and Confidence

1. What is Self-Esteem?

Self-esteem refers to the overall sense of self-worth and self-acceptance. It reflects how individuals perceive their abilities, values, and relationships. A strong self-esteem foundation helps adolescents feel capable and valued, whereas low self-esteem can lead to self-doubt, insecurity, and emotional distress.

2. What is Confidence?

Confidence is the belief in one's ability to accomplish tasks and face challenges. It enables adolescents to take risks, express themselves assertively, and persist in the face of adversity. Confidence grows through experiences, achievements, and overcoming obstacles.

3. The Relationship Between Self-Esteem and Confidence

Self-esteem and confidence are interconnected but distinct. A person with high self-esteem generally feels worthy and valuable, whereas confidence relates to specific skills and capabilities. A balanced combination of both contributes to personal growth and well-being.

Factors Influencing Self-Esteem and Confidence

Several factors shape an adolescent's self-esteem and confidence levels:

1. Family and Upbringing

- Supportive parenting fosters a sense of security and self-worth.
- Negative criticism or unrealistic expectations can lower self-esteem.

2. Peer Influence and Social Relationships

- Positive friendships encourage self-expression and validation.
- Bullying, exclusion, or comparison to others can diminish confidence.

3. Academic Performance and Achievements

- Success in school and extracurricular activities boosts confidence.
- Fear of failure or underachievement can cause self-doubt.

4. Body Image and Media Influence

- Unrealistic beauty standards on social media affect self-perception.
- Accepting one's unique features fosters self-esteem.

5. Personal Mindset and Self-Talk

- Positive affirmations and a growth mindset build confidence.
- Negative self-criticism erodes self-worth.

The Impact of Low Self-Esteem and Poor Confidence

Adolescents with low self-esteem may experience:

- Social withdrawal and reluctance to engage in activities.
- Increased anxiety, stress, and depression.
- Difficulty asserting themselves or handling criticism.
- Risk-taking behaviours to seek approval or validation.

Conversely, healthy self-esteem promotes:

- Resilience in handling challenges and setbacks.
- Better decision-making and problem-solving skills.
- Positive social interactions and leadership qualities.

Strategies for Building Self-Esteem and Confidence

1. Practicing Self-Compassion and Positive Self-Talk

- Replace self-criticism with encouraging words.
- Recognize personal strengths and accomplishments.

2. Setting Realistic Goals and Celebrating Achievements

- Break tasks into manageable steps to experience success.
- Reward progress, no matter how small, to boost confidence.

3. Developing a Growth Mindset

- Embrace challenges as opportunities to learn and improve.
- Understand that abilities can be developed through effort and perseverance.

4. Engaging in Activities That Foster Confidence

- Pursue hobbies and interests that bring joy and accomplishment.
- Join clubs, sports, or creative groups to build social skills and self-worth.

5. Building Healthy Relationships

- Surround oneself with supportive and uplifting people.
- Avoid toxic friendships that undermine confidence.

6. Limiting Social Media Comparison

- Focus on personal growth rather than external validation.
- Unfollow accounts that promote unrealistic beauty standards.

7. Practicing Assertiveness and Communication Skills

- Express opinions and needs confidently and respectfully.
- Stand up for oneself without aggression or passivity.

8. Prioritizing Self-Care and Well-Being

- Maintain a balanced lifestyle with proper sleep, nutrition, and exercise.
- Engage in relaxation techniques such as mindfulness or journaling.

Overcoming Self-Doubt and Fear of Failure

Adolescents may struggle with self-doubt when facing challenges. Strategies to overcome these fears include:

- Viewing failure as a learning experience rather than a personal flaw.
- Practicing resilience by bouncing back from setbacks.
- Seeking guidance from mentors or role models for encouragement.

Seeking Support and Professional Help

In cases where self-esteem issues significantly impact daily life, seeking professional guidance can be beneficial. Therapists, counsellors, or support groups can provide strategies for building confidence and self-worth.

Conclusion

Building self-esteem and confidence is a continuous journey that requires self-awareness, positive habits, and supportive relationships. By embracing self-acceptance, setting goals, and developing a resilient mindset, adolescents can cultivate a strong sense of self-worth and lead fulfilling lives. Encouraging self-confidence early on lays the foundation for long-term success and happiness.

CHAPTER XVI

EFFECTIVE COMMUNICATION SKILLS

Introduction

Communication is a fundamental aspect of human interaction, influencing relationships, career success, and personal growth. Effective communication skills enable individuals to express their thoughts clearly, build meaningful relationships, and resolve conflicts constructively. For adolescents, developing strong communication abilities is essential for navigating social interactions, academic environments, and future professional settings.

This chapter explores the principles of effective communication, types of communication, common barriers, and practical strategies to enhance verbal, non-verbal, and written communication skills.

Understanding Communication

1. What is Communication?

Communication is the process of exchanging information, thoughts, and feelings between individuals through verbal, non-verbal, and written methods. Effective communication involves both sending and receiving messages accurately and meaningfully.

2. The Importance of Effective Communication

- Builds Strong Relationships: Good communication fosters trust and understanding in personal and professional relationships.
- Enhances Academic and Career Success: Clear communication is vital for academic achievement, teamwork, and workplace interactions.
- Promotes Conflict Resolution: Effective communicators can address conflicts calmly and find solutions collaboratively.

- Boosts Self-Confidence: Articulating thoughts clearly helps individuals feel more confident in social and professional settings.

Types of Communication

1. Verbal Communication

Verbal communication includes spoken words, tone of voice, and clarity of speech. Key aspects include:

- Clarity and Conciseness: Expressing thoughts clearly and avoiding unnecessary information.
- Active Listening: Paying attention, paraphrasing, and responding thoughtfully.
- Tone and Inflection: Using appropriate tone to convey emotions effectively.

2. Non-Verbal Communication

Non-verbal cues, such as facial expressions, gestures, and body language, play a crucial role in communication. Effective use of non-verbal communication includes:

- Maintaining Eye Contact: Signifies confidence and attentiveness.
- Appropriate Gestures: Enhances verbal messages and adds emphasis.
- Posture and Proximity: Conveys openness and engagement.

3. Written Communication

Written communication is essential for academic, professional, and personal correspondence. Key elements of effective writing include:

- Clear Structure: Organizing ideas logically.
- Proper Grammar and Punctuation: Enhancing readability and professionalism.
- Concise Messaging: Avoiding unnecessary details and maintaining clarity.

Common Barriers to Effective Communication

Despite its importance, several factors can hinder communication:

- Language and Cultural Differences: Misinterpretations due to linguistic or cultural variances.
- Emotional Barriers: Anxiety, fear, or anger affecting clarity.
- Distractions and Noise: Environmental or mental distractions disrupting message reception.
- Lack of Confidence: Hesitation or fear of judgment leading to ineffective communication.

Strategies to Improve Communication Skills

1. Active Listening

Listening is just as important as speaking. To become a better listener:

- Give Full Attention: Avoid distractions and focus on the speaker.
- Show Engagement: Use nodding, facial expressions, and brief verbal affirmations.
- Ask Clarifying Questions: Ensures understanding and encourages open dialogue.

2. Enhancing Verbal Skills

- Think Before Speaking: Organize thoughts before verbalizing them.

- Use Simple and Direct Language: Avoid jargon and overly complex sentences.
- Practice Public Speaking: Helps build confidence and fluency.

3. Improving Non-Verbal Communication

- Be Aware of Body Language: Maintain an open posture and avoid defensive gestures.
- Regulate Facial Expressions: Ensure expressions match the intended message.
- Use Gestures to Reinforce Speech: Complement words with appropriate hand movements.

4. Strengthening Written Communication

- Plan Before Writing: Outline key points to ensure logical flow.
- Edit and Proofread: Check for errors and refine clarity.
- Use Appropriate Tone: Match the tone to the audience and purpose.

5. Building Confidence in Communication

- Practice Regularly: Engage in conversations and public speaking opportunities.
- Seek Feedback: Ask for constructive criticism to improve.
- Develop a Growth Mindset: View communication challenges as learning opportunities.

The Role of Technology in Modern Communication

With advancements in technology, communication has evolved significantly. While digital platforms provide convenience, they also present challenges:

- Advantages: Instant messaging, global connectivity, and access to information.
- Challenges: Misinterpretation of tone in texts, over-reliance on digital interactions, and decreased face-to-face communication skills.

To use technology effectively:

- Maintain a Balance: Limit screen time and engage in real-life interactions.
- Be Mindful of Online Etiquette: Use respectful language and avoid misunderstandings.
- Develop Digital Literacy: Understand the impact of online communication and social media.

Effective Communication in Different Settings

1. Communication in Personal Relationships

- Express Feelings Honestly: Open and honest dialogue strengthens relationships.
- Practice Empathy: Understand and validate others' perspectives.
- Resolve Conflicts Peacefully: Use active listening and compromise to address issues.

2. Communication in the Workplace

- Be Professional and Respectful: Maintain courtesy in interactions.
- Collaborate Effectively: Foster teamwork through clear discussions.

- Give and Receive Feedback: Constructive criticism helps growth and improvement.

3. Communication in Academic Environments

- Participate in Discussions: Engage in classroom activities and express ideas confidently.
- Ask for Help When Needed: Clarify doubts by seeking assistance from teachers or peers.
- Practice Presentation Skills: Develop strong public speaking techniques for academic success.

Conclusion

Effective communication skills are vital for personal, academic, and professional success. By developing verbal, non-verbal, and written communication abilities, individuals can express themselves clearly, build strong relationships, and navigate social and professional interactions with confidence. Practicing active listening, refining speech clarity, and utilizing digital communication responsibly can enhance communication effectiveness. Mastering these skills empowers individuals to connect meaningfully with others and achieve their goals.

CHAPTER XVII

TIME MANAGEMENT AND PRODUCTIVITY

Introduction

Time management is a crucial skill that allows individuals to make the most of their available time, improve efficiency, and achieve their personal and professional goals. Adolescents, in particular, often struggle with balancing academics, extracurricular activities, social interactions, and personal responsibilities. Developing strong time management skills not only enhances productivity but also reduces stress, improves mental health, and fosters a sense of accomplishment.

This chapter explores the fundamentals of time management, the relationship between time management and productivity, common obstacles, and practical strategies to optimize time utilization.

Understanding Time Management

1. What is Time Management?

Time management refers to the ability to plan, prioritize, and execute tasks effectively within a set timeframe. It involves setting goals, allocating resources, minimizing distractions, and tracking progress to enhance efficiency.

2. The Importance of Effective Time Management

- Boosts Productivity: Maximizing output in minimal time improves overall efficiency.
- Reduces Stress: Proper planning prevents last-minute rushes and anxiety.
- Enhances Academic and Professional Success: Meeting deadlines and managing workload effectively leads to better performance.

- Promotes Work-Life Balance: Allocating time appropriately ensures a balance between work, studies, and personal life.

The Relationship Between Time Management and Productivity

Productivity is the measure of how efficiently an individual completes tasks within a given timeframe. Effective time management directly contributes to enhanced productivity by helping individuals:

- Set clear priorities to focus on important tasks.
- Avoid procrastination by breaking tasks into manageable segments.
- Utilize time blocks for focused work sessions.
- Develop discipline in following a structured schedule.

Common Barriers to Time Management

Despite its significance, many individuals face challenges in managing their time effectively:

- Procrastination: Delaying tasks leads to last-minute stress and lower-quality work.
- Poor Planning: Lack of a structured plan results in missed deadlines and inefficiency.
- Multitasking: Attempting multiple tasks at once reduces focus and productivity.
- Distractions: social media, television, and unplanned interruptions disrupt workflow.
- Lack of Motivation: Low energy levels and lack of purpose hinder productivity.

Strategies for Effective Time Management

1. Setting Clear Goals and Priorities

- Define SMART Goals: Ensure goals are Specific, Measurable, Achievable, Relevant, and Time-bound.
- Prioritize Tasks: Use techniques like the Eisenhower Matrix to distinguish between urgent and important tasks.
- Break Goals into Smaller Steps: Completing small milestones makes large tasks more manageable.

2. Planning and Scheduling

- Create a Daily or Weekly Planner: Outline tasks in advance to stay organized.
- Use Time Blocks: Allocate specific time slots for focused work.
- Set Realistic Deadlines: Avoid overloading the schedule with unrealistic expectations.

3. Avoiding Procrastination

- Use the Pomodoro Technique: Work in short bursts with breaks to maintain focus.
- Eliminate Distractions: Turn off notifications and create a dedicated workspace.
- Set Short-Term Rewards: Reward yourself upon task completion to stay motivated.

4. Enhancing Focus and Productivity

- Practice Mindfulness: Being present while working improves concentration.
- Use Productivity Tools: Apps like Trello, Todoist, and Notion help in organizing tasks.
- Adopt the Two-Minute Rule: If a task takes less than two minutes, do it immediately.

5. Developing a Routine and Discipline

- Start the Day with a Plan: Having a morning routine sets the tone for a productive day.
- Stick to Consistent Work Hours: Consistency enhances efficiency and reduces wasted time.
- Review and Reflect: Assess what worked and adjust strategies accordingly.

Balancing Work and Leisure

While productivity is essential, overworking can lead to burnout. Maintaining a balance between work and personal life is crucial.

- Schedule Breaks: Taking short breaks enhances creativity and prevents mental fatigue.
- Engage in Recreational Activities: Exercise, hobbies, and social interactions promote overall well-being.
- Practice Self-Care: Prioritizing sleep, nutrition, and relaxation contributes to sustained productivity.

Technology and Time Management

Technology can be a double-edged sword. When used wisely, it enhances efficiency, but excessive use can lead to distractions.

- Use Productivity Apps: Digital planners, timers, and goal-setting apps optimize workflow.
- Limit Social Media Consumption: Set boundaries to prevent excessive scrolling and distractions.
- Automate Repetitive Tasks: Utilize automation tools to save time on routine activities.

Time Management in Different Aspects of Life

1. Academic Time Management

- Create a Study Schedule: Allocate time for each subject to avoid last-minute cramming.
- Take Effective Notes: Summarize key points to review information quickly.
- Prepare for Exams in Advance: Avoid procrastination by setting study milestones.

2. Professional Time Management

- Set Career Goals: Define professional milestones and create an action plan.
- Manage Emails Efficiently: Allocate specific times for checking emails.
- Prioritize Networking and Skill Development: Continuous learning enhances career prospects.

3. Personal Time Management

- Practice Mindful Living: Be intentional about how time is spent.
- Set Boundaries: Learn to say no to commitments that don't align with priorities.

- Plan Leisure Activities: Allocate time for hobbies and relaxation.

Overcoming Time Management Challenges

When facing time management difficulties, individuals can:

- Reassess Priorities: Adjust schedules to focus on what truly matters.
- Seek Guidance: Mentors, coaches, or self-help books can provide valuable insights.
- Develop Resilience: Accept setbacks and learn from mistakes without self-judgment.

Conclusion

Effective time management is a key skill that contributes to personal and professional success. By setting clear goals, eliminating distractions, and maintaining a structured schedule, individuals can optimize their productivity and well-being. Whether managing academic responsibilities, professional commitments, or personal tasks, mastering time management enhances efficiency, reduces stress, and promotes a fulfilling life.

CHAPTER XVIII

SETTING GOALS FOR PERSONAL DEVELOPEMENTS

Setting goals is a powerful tool for personal growth and success. Goals provide direction, motivation, and a sense of purpose, helping individuals achieve their aspirations in various aspects of life. Whether in academics, career, health, or personal relationships, having clear goals enhances focus, productivity, and overall well-being.

This chapter explores the importance of goal setting, different types of goals, effective goal-setting strategies, overcoming obstacles, and maintaining motivation. By mastering the art of goal setting, individuals can create a structured approach to achieving their dreams and maximizing their potential.

The Importance of Goal Setting

1. Provides Direction and Focus

Goals act as a roadmap, guiding individuals toward their desired outcomes. Without a clear goal, efforts can become scattered and unproductive. Establishing specific objectives ensures a structured approach to achieving success.

2. Enhances Motivation

Having a goal fosters a sense of purpose and keeps individuals motivated to stay committed. Goals provide something to strive for, increasing determination and persistence.

3. Improves Time Management

Well-defined goals help in prioritizing tasks and managing time efficiently. Setting deadlines and breaking down tasks into smaller steps ensures steady progress.

4. Builds Self-Discipline and Resilience

Working towards a goal requires commitment, patience, and perseverance. Overcoming obstacles along the way strengthens resilience and fosters personal growth.

5. Measures Progress and Success

Tracking progress toward a goal allows individuals to assess their growth and make necessary adjustments. Celebrating small achievements along the way reinforces motivation.

Types of Goals

1. Short-Term Goals

Short-term goals are immediate objectives that can be accomplished within days, weeks, or months. Examples include:

- Completing a book within a month
- Exercising daily for 30 minutes
- Improving study habits for an upcoming exam

2. Long-Term Goals

Long-term goals take years to achieve and require consistent effort. Examples include:

- Earning a college degree
- Advancing in a chosen career path
- Maintaining a healthy lifestyle over the years

3. Personal Development Goals

These goals focus on self-improvement, enhancing skills, and achieving personal growth. Examples include:

- Developing better communication skills
- Cultivating a positive mindset
- Learning a new language

4. Career and Educational Goals

These goals help individuals achieve success in their professional and academic journeys. Examples include:

- Securing an internship in a desired field
- Achieving a specific GPA
- Gaining expertise in a particular subject

5. Financial Goals

Financial planning is essential for long-term stability and security. Examples include:

- Saving a certain amount of money each month
- Investing in assets for future financial growth
- Creating and sticking to a budget

Effective Goal-Setting Strategies

1. SMART Goals Approach

The SMART framework ensures that goals are:

- Specific: Clearly defined and focused

- Measurable: Quantifiable progress tracking
- Achievable: Realistic within available resources
- Relevant: Aligning with overall objectives
- Time-Bound: Having a deadline for accomplishment

2. Writing Goals Down

Documenting goals enhances commitment and accountability. Keeping a written record of objectives reinforces motivation.

3. Breaking Goals into Smaller Steps

Large goals can feel overwhelming. Breaking them into smaller, manageable tasks makes progress more attainable.

4. Prioritizing Goals

Focusing on the most important goals prevents distractions and improves time management.

5. Developing an Action Plan

Creating a step-by-step approach ensures a clear path toward achieving a goal.

Overcoming Obstacles to Goal Achievement

1. Fear of Failure

Many individuals avoid setting goals due to the fear of not achieving them. Viewing failures as learning experiences fosters growth and resilience.

2. Lack of Motivation

Staying motivated can be challenging. Surrounding oneself with supportive peers, visualizing success, and celebrating small achievements can boost motivation.

3. Procrastination

Postponing tasks delays progress. Implementing time management techniques like the Pomodoro Technique can help combat procrastination.

4. External Challenges

Life circumstances can sometimes hinder progress. Adjusting goals when necessary ensures flexibility while maintaining determination.

Maintaining Motivation and Commitment

1. Tracking Progress

Regularly assessing progress helps in staying on track. Using journals or digital tracking apps can be effective.

2. Seeking Support and Accountability

Sharing goals with mentors, friends, or family members provides encouragement and accountability.

3. Visualizing Success

Imagining the outcome of achieving a goal reinforces commitment and determination.

4. Rewarding Milestones

Celebrating small successes boosts morale and encourages continued effort.

Conclusion

Goal setting is a crucial skill that fosters personal growth, motivation, and success. By setting clear, realistic objectives and implementing effective strategies, individuals can unlock their full potential. Overcoming obstacles, maintaining commitment, and tracking progress ensure long-term achievements. Developing strong goal-setting habits early in life paves the way for a fulfilling and purposeful journey toward success.

CHAPTER XIX

PREPARING FOR ADULTHOOD, CAREER AND SKILLS

Adulthood marks a major transition in life that comes with increased independence, responsibilities, and challenges. Many adolescents find themselves unprepared for the complexities of adult life, including career decisions, financial management, and self-sufficiency. To navigate adulthood successfully, it is essential to develop critical life skills and make informed decisions regarding career paths, financial stability, and personal growth.

This chapter explores the essential skills required for a smooth transition into adulthood, focusing on career planning, financial literacy, personal development, and emotional resilience.

Understanding Adulthood and Its Challenges

1. The Shift from Adolescence to Adulthood

- Increased responsibilities and independence
- Importance of decision-making and accountability
- Developing a long-term vision for the future

2. Common Challenges Young Adults Face

- Managing finances and budgeting
- Adapting to workplace culture
- Building and maintaining relationships
- Handling stress and mental well-being
- Balancing personal and professional life

Career Planning and Professional Development

1. Choosing the Right Career Path

- Identifying interests, strengths, and skills
- Researching potential career opportunities
- The importance of internships and volunteer work

2. Resume Writing and Job Applications

- How to create a compelling resume
- Writing effective cover letters
- Tips for standing out in job applications

3. Preparing for Job Interviews

- Common interview questions and how to answer them
- The importance of confidence and communication skills
- Dressing professionally and making a good first impression

4. Workplace Etiquette and Professionalism

- Understanding workplace dynamics
- Time management and meeting deadlines
- Respectful communication with colleagues and supervisors

Financial Literacy and Money Management

1. Budgeting and Expense Management

- Creating a monthly budget
- Differentiating between needs and wants
- Managing unexpected expenses

2. Understanding Credit and Loans

- How credit scores work
- Responsible use of credit cards
- Understanding student loans and repayment options

3. Savings and Investment Strategies

- The importance of saving early
- Introduction to investment options (stocks, bonds, mutual funds)
- Planning for long-term financial security

Personal Development and Self-Sufficiency

1. Time Management and Organization

- Prioritizing tasks effectively
- Creating a daily and weekly schedule
- Avoiding procrastination and staying focused

2. Decision-Making and Problem-Solving Skills

- Analysing situations before making decisions
- Learning from mistakes and experiences
- Developing critical thinking skills

3. Emotional Intelligence and Resilience

- Managing emotions in difficult situations
- Developing empathy and understanding others
- Handling stress and setbacks with resilience

Building Healthy Relationships and Social Skills

1. Effective Communication in Adulthood

- Verbal and non-verbal communication skills
- Active listening and conflict resolution
- Maintaining professional and personal relationships

2. Networking and Social Connections

- The importance of building a strong network
- How to approach networking events
- Leveraging social media for career growth

3. Balancing Work and Personal Life

- Setting boundaries for a healthy lifestyle
- The importance of relaxation and self-care
- Maintaining meaningful relationships while pursuing goals

Conclusion

Preparing for adulthood requires a proactive approach to career planning, financial management, personal development, and social interactions. By developing essential life skills, young adults can confidently transition into independence and build a successful future. Taking responsibility for one's growth and making informed decisions will lead to a fulfilling and well-balanced life

CHAPTER XX

MINDFULLNESS AND MEDITATION

Introduction

Mindfulness and meditation have been practiced for centuries as tools to cultivate self-awareness, emotional balance, and mental clarity. In modern times, they have gained popularity as essential practices for reducing stress, improving focus, and enhancing overall well-being. Adolescents and young adults, who often face academic pressure, social expectations, and personal challenges, can significantly benefit from incorporating mindfulness and meditation into their daily lives.

This chapter explores the principles of mindfulness, the benefits of meditation, different techniques, and practical ways to integrate mindfulness into daily routines. By understanding and practicing these skills, individuals can develop resilience, increase self-awareness, and improve their mental and emotional well-being.

Understanding Mindfulness

1. What is Mindfulness?

Mindfulness is the practice of being fully present in the moment, aware of thoughts, emotions, and sensations without judgment. It involves consciously directing attention to the present experience rather than dwelling on the past or worrying about the future.

2. The Science Behind Mindfulness

Scientific studies have shown that mindfulness affects the brain in positive ways, including:

- Enhancing neural pathways associated with emotional regulation.

- Reducing activity in the amygdala, which controls stress and fear responses.
- Increasing the density of grey matter in areas related to learning, memory, and self-awareness.

3. Benefits of Mindfulness

Practicing mindfulness regularly leads to numerous benefits, such as:

- Improved Focus and Concentration: Helps in academic and professional success.
- Stress Reduction: Lowers cortisol levels, the hormone responsible for stress.
- Enhanced Emotional Regulation: Encourages thoughtful responses instead of impulsive reactions.
- Better Sleep Quality: Reduces insomnia and enhances restful sleep.
- Increased Self-Awareness: Promotes a deeper understanding of thoughts and behaviours.

Understanding Meditation

1. What is Meditation?

Meditation is a structured practice that trains the mind to achieve mental clarity, relaxation, and inner peace. It involves techniques such as breathing exercises, guided visualization, and focused attention.

2. Different Types of Meditation

Several forms of meditation exist, each with unique benefits:

- Mindfulness Meditation: Focusing on breath or bodily sensations to remain present.
- Loving-Kindness Meditation: Cultivating compassion and positive emotions.

- Guided Meditation: Following verbal instructions to visualize calming scenarios.
- Transcendental Meditation: Using mantras to reach a state of deep relaxation.
- Movement-Based Meditation: Practices like yoga and tai chi that integrate mindfulness with physical activity.

3. How Meditation Changes the Brain

Research shows that meditation leads to long-term changes in brain structure and function, including:

- Thicker Prefrontal Cortex: Enhances decision-making and self-control.
- Increased Hippocampal Volume: Supports memory and learning.
- Stronger Connections Between Brain Hemispheres: Improves cognitive flexibility and emotional stability.

Practical Strategies for Integrating Mindfulness and Meditation

1. Developing a Mindful Morning Routine

- Start the day with a few minutes of deep breathing or meditation.
- Practice gratitude by reflecting on positive aspects of life.
- Avoid digital distractions in the first hour after waking up.

2. Mindful Eating

- Pay attention to textures, flavours, and sensations while eating.
- Avoid distractions like watching TV or scrolling on the phone during meals.
- Chew slowly and appreciate the nourishment provided by food.

3. Practicing Mindfulness Throughout the Day

- Take short breaks to observe surroundings and connect with the present moment.
- Use mindfulness techniques while commuting, studying, or working.
- Set reminders to pause and take deep breaths periodically.

4. Evening Meditation for Relaxation

- Engage in a guided meditation or breathing exercises before bedtime.
- Reflect on the day without judgment, acknowledging successes and areas for improvement.
- Maintain a journal to track progress and emotions related to mindfulness practice.

Overcoming Challenges in Practicing Mindfulness and Meditation

1. Dealing with a Busy Mind

- Understand that wandering thoughts are natural; gently bring attention back to the present.
- Start with short sessions and gradually increase duration.

2. Staying Consistent

- Establish a specific time each day for mindfulness or meditation.
- Use apps or guided sessions to stay motivated and structured.

3. Managing Scepticism and Resistance

- Recognize the scientifically proven benefits of mindfulness.
- Approach the practice with an open mind and patience.

The Role of Mindfulness in Emotional and Mental Well-Being

1. Enhancing Emotional Intelligence

- Develops self-awareness, self-regulation, and empathy.
- Strengthens interpersonal relationships through better communication and understanding.

2. Coping with Anxiety and Stress

- Mindfulness helps individuals observe anxious thoughts without reacting negatively.
- Meditation lowers stress hormones, promoting relaxation and balance.

3. Improving Decision-Making and Resilience

- Encourages thoughtful responses to challenges instead of impulsive reactions.
- Builds the ability to remain calm and focused during difficult situations.

Conclusion

Mindfulness and meditation offer powerful tools for enhancing mental clarity, emotional resilience, and overall well-being. By incorporating these practices into daily life, individuals can improve their focus, manage stress effectively, and cultivate a deeper sense of inner peace. Whether through simple breathing exercises, guided meditation, or mindful living, the benefits of these techniques are long-lasting and transformative. Embracing mindfulness and meditation can lead to a more balanced, fulfilling life, paving the way for personal growth and self-discovery.

CHAPTER XXI

IMMUNIZATION DURING ADOLESCENCE

Importance of Adolescent Immunization

Immunization during adolescence is crucial in protecting individuals from infectious diseases that can have long-term health consequences. Vaccinations at this stage help in boosting immunity against diseases that may not have been fully covered in childhood. Additionally, adolescent immunization plays a significant role in maintaining herd immunity, preventing outbreaks, and reducing the overall burden of vaccine-preventable diseases.

Vaccine-Preventable Diseases

Adolescents are susceptible to various vaccine-preventable diseases, including human papillomavirus (HPV), meningococcal infections, influenza, tetanus, diphtheria, and pertussis. These diseases can lead to severe complications, long-term health issues, and even fatalities. Immunization provides an effective shield against these diseases, ensuring better health outcomes and reducing the risk of transmission within communities.

Key Vaccines for Adolescents

Several vaccines are recommended during adolescence to provide continued protection and prevent new infections. The key vaccines include:

- HPV Vaccine: Protects against cervical and other HPV-related cancers.
- Meningococcal Vaccine: Prevents bacterial meningitis and related complications.
- Tdap Vaccine: Provides immunity against tetanus, diphtheria, and pertussis.
- Influenza Vaccine: Recommended annually to guard against flu strains.
- Hepatitis B Vaccine: Essential in preventing chronic liver disease and liver cancer.

HPV Vaccine and Cervical Cancer Prevention

The HPV vaccine is one of the most important immunizations for adolescents, especially for preventing cervical cancer. Human papillomavirus is a leading cause of cervical and other cancers, and early vaccination provides the best protection. The vaccine is administered in two or three doses, depending on the age of initiation. Countries with widespread HPV vaccination programs have witnessed a significant reduction in cervical cancer cases, emphasizing its effectiveness in disease prevention.

Types of HPV Vaccines:

- Gardasil-9: Protects against nine HPV types, including those causing cervical, vaginal, vulvar, and anal cancers, as well as genital warts.
- Gardasil: Covers four HPV types and prevents cervical cancer and genital warts.
- Cervarix: Focuses on preventing cervical cancer by protecting against the most high-risk HPV strains.

Who Should Get Vaccinated?

- Recommended for both boys and girls, ideally between ages 9-14.
- Catch-up vaccination is available up to age 26.
- Some guidelines suggest vaccination for adults up to age 45 based on risk factors.

Effectiveness and Safety:

- Studies show over 90% effectiveness in preventing HPV-related cancers.
- The vaccine has undergone rigorous safety testing and is continuously monitored.
- Common side effects include mild pain at the injection site, headache, and fatigue.

Global and National Vaccination Programs

Various global and national initiatives aim to improve adolescent immunization rates, particularly for the HPV vaccine. The World Health Organization (WHO) has set targets to eliminate cervical cancer through widespread HPV vaccination. Organizations such as GAVI, the Vaccine Alliance support immunization efforts in low-income countries. Many governments have also introduced school-based vaccination programs to ensure accessibility and higher coverage rates among adolescents.

Strategies to Improve Coverage

Despite the availability of vaccines, immunization coverage remains a challenge in some regions due to misinformation, vaccine hesitancy, and logistical barriers. Strategies to improve coverage include:

- Public Awareness Campaigns: Educating communities about the benefits of adolescent immunization.
- School-Based Vaccination Programs: Making vaccines accessible through educational institutions.
- Healthcare Provider Advocacy: Encouraging doctors and nurses to promote vaccinations.
- Combating Misinformation: Addressing vaccine myths through factual information and outreach efforts.

Immunization during adolescence is a critical public health strategy that safeguards individual and community health. By ensuring high vaccine coverage and addressing barriers, the risk of vaccine-preventable diseases can be significantly minimized, leading to a healthier future generation.

References

1. National Institute of Mental Health and Neurosciences (NIMHANS) (2020). Mental Health and Adolescence in India. Bangalore, India.
2. Indian Council of Medical Research (ICMR) (2019). Nutritional Needs of Adolescents: An Indian Perspective.
3. Ministry of Health and Family Welfare, Government of India (2021). National Guidelines on Digital Health and Adolescent Well-being.
4. Taneja, V., & Sharma, R. (2022). "Impact of Social Media on Adolescent Mental Health in India." Indian Journal of Psychiatry, 64(3), 215-228.
5. Kumar, P., & Agarwal, S. (2021). "Physical Activity Trends in Indian Adolescents: A Cross-Sectional Study." Journal of Public Health Research and Development, 12(2), 145-160.
6. Gupta, A., & Mishra, D. (2020). "Sleep Hygiene and Academic Performance among Indian Teenagers." Indian Journal of Sleep Research, 6(1), 80-95.
7. All India Institute of Medical Sciences (AIIMS) (2021). Stress and Anxiety Among Adolescents: A National Study.

1. World Health Organization (WHO) (2021). Adolescent Health and Well-being: Global Report.
2. American Psychological Association (APA) (2020). "Cognitive Development and Stress Management in Adolescents." Journal of Adolescent Psychology, 45(4), 303-319.
3. National Sleep Foundation (NSF) (2019). Sleep Hygiene and Teen Development: A Global Perspective.
4. Centres for Disease Control and Prevention (CDC) (2021). "Substance Abuse Prevention Strategies for Adolescents." Journal of Adolescent Health, 68(2), 122-137.
5. Harvard Medical School (2022). "The Neuroscience of Adolescent Brain Development." Harvard Review of Psychiatry, 30(1), 45-60.
6. Stanford University Mindfulness Research Centre (2021). "Meditation and Mindfulness: Effects on Teen Stress and Focus." Journal of Mind-Body Medicine, 18(2), 90-112.
7. United Nations Children's Fund (UNICEF) (2020). Digital Well-being and Online Safety for Youth.

REFERENCES

8. British Journal of Sports Medicine (2019). "The Role of Physical Activity in Adolescence: A Longitudinal Study."
9. Johns Hopkins Bloomberg School of Public Health (2021). "Emotional Intelligence and Resilience Among Adolescents." Journal of Child Development, 77(5), 345-360.
10. University of California, Berkeley (2020). "Time Management and Productivity Techniques for Adolescents." Journal of Applied Psychology, 55(3), 200-220.
11. Cambridge University Press (2019). The Role of Nutrition in Adolescent Development: A Global Review.